NOTHING EVER HAPPENS HERE

Graham Vickers

Nothing Ever Happens Here
by Graham Vickers

First published in Great Britain in 2020.

Typeset by Eleanor Abraham,
using Adobe Garamond Pro and Domus Titling.

Produced on paper from sustainable sources.

A CIP catalogue record for this title is
available from the British Library.

Cover photographs:
Jane Coltman – Rothbury Riverside –
permission from *Northumberland Gazette*.
Mary Scott – Rothbury police and
community – with permission.

email: grahamavickers@icloud.com
Twitter: @grahamavickers
www.nothingeverhappenshere.uk

ISBNs
Print: 978 1 8382403 0 1
eBook: 978 1 8382403 1 8

CONTENTS

PREFACE

Manhunts involving armed and dangerous criminals are extremely rare in the UK. In July 2010, a domestic revenge killing in the North East of England led to one of the biggest police manhunts in British history. The Raoul Moat incident brought terror to an isolated Northumberland community; the media was animated, the nation gripped.

In the early hours of Saturday, 3 July, in Birtley, Gateshead, Moat shot and executed Christopher Brown, the new partner of his ex-girlfriend Samantha Stobbart. The gunman then turned the shotgun on Stobbart, blasting the gun through the lounge window and leaving her for dead. Moat fled the scene.

Several hours later, the gunman inflicted further revenge by shooting unarmed Northumbria Police Constable David Rathband in the face while the officer was stationary in his patrol car. PC Rathband suffered permanent loss of sight, which ended in personal tragedy. Moat remained at large, threatening to kill police officers as the seven-day police hunt for him unfolded.

Just days previously – in my role as neighbourhood sergeant in the remote rural village of Rothbury, Northumberland – 'nothing ever happens here' were the words I had used to describe Rothbury to visiting police colleagues. Now those words couldn't have been further from the truth, as an armed Moat entered the village, threatening not only to shoot police officers, but to kill innocent members of the public. Rothbury was sealed off and residents placed under lockdown, with more than 160 firearms officers, from 18 police forces, deployed. The world's media descended on the close-knit community as rural tranquillity turned to turmoil. The manhunt for Raoul Moat focused the eyes of the world on a village under siege.

In Rothbury I was uniquely placed at the hub of local policing and the community. I observed the challenges, the fears of officers, and the frustrations of the community as Moat remained elusive. *Nothing Ever Happens Here* presents a detailed account of the manhunt in Rothbury, which led to his capture, stand-off and death. I provide a perspective of the aftermath, as normality returned; a personal account of the various trials, inquiries and inquests. I explore the madness of the media, and I depict the best and worst in human nature, which determined the fate of the many people involved. As a passionate believer in neighbourhood policing, I unashamedly defend community policing during the austere years that followed. *Nothing Ever Happens Here* concludes with reflection and pride: in the force, police officers and the community.

At no time following the event did I ever consider writing a community policing perspective of the Moat incident. Such a task was alien in thought; however, following a visit to the air support unit at Newcastle Airport to show my young children the force helicopter, it dawned on me that as soon as I mentioned my posting at Rothbury, everyone, without exception, had either some involvement, an insight or a story to tell of the incident. Recollections came from the helicopter observer, firearms officer, negotiator, force media adviser, senior police officer, resident, baker or whoever; they all had their own memories and experiences to tell.

My personal narrative was strengthened by listening to the many accounts of the officers, residents and people involved. Everyone willingly and openly shared their recollections of the event. Their truths, whether accurate, factual, opinion or otherwise, enable the book to present the best obtainable version of events.

While a plethora of Moat articles have been written, and television programmes produced, such content has overly focused on Moat, firearms, senior detectives and chief officers. There appeared scant regard for the community and the involvement of the neighbourhood policing team, who were instrumental in bringing the incident to a conclusion. By adopting a more balanced rural policing narrative, critical concerns are openly highlighted, humanity is expressed without glorification, and dignity shown to all victims.

Nothing Ever Happens Here provides a unique 'bottom-up' policing and community perspective. The Moat incident will slowly fade into the annals of history, with only memories and innuendo passing down through the generations. This book will provide one of the most authoritative accounts of the Raoul Moat manhunt in Rothbury, and reflect how the police and community came together in the face of adversity.

Graham Vickers

1
NOTHING EVER HAPPENS HERE

While I was completing paperwork in the back room of Rothbury Police Station in late June 2010, as a beautiful summer's day beckoned, the station buzzer sounded to alert me to the presence of visitors at the front counter. I walked through to the front office, where three burly, middle-aged men stood in the public foyer, dressed in black combat clothing. The man in the centre was shorter than the two burly men either side of him – one balding, the other with spiked ginger hair – and together they gave the appearance of pub bouncers from Newcastle.

The men identified themselves as Northumbria Police Training Department staff who had travelled from force headquarters. Their mission? To undertake a risk assessment of our police office to ensure its suitability for use by police volunteers to meet and greet the public. I smiled.

'What? The three of you to risk-assess a little police office?'

They all grinned sheepishly. 'It's a lovely sunny day,' one remarked.

'Nothing ever happens here,' I pointed out, as I invited them through to the back room to put the kettle on.

As a matter of fact, I was pleased to have police visitors. In remote rural areas you can sometimes feel isolated from colleagues, unlike in towns and cities. To have some police civilisation was welcome, if only to catch up on events elsewhere in the force, and on any gossip. Nothing happens at Rothbury in comparison to other police areas. Having served in the Metropolitan Police at Finchley during the Thatcher years, I transferred to Northumbria Police in 1992, where I worked in various roles: 24/7 police response; criminal justice research; custody officer; and as a sergeant at Communications, responsible for overseeing critical incidents. In 2008 I was posted to Rothbury as the neighbourhood sergeant.

Policing Rothbury and the Coquet Valley had its occasional challenges. The River Coquet burst its banks in 2008, causing several homes to be flooded and the residents evacuated. In 2009, disruption to gas supplies over several days of freezing winter weather left hundreds of Rothbury residents vulnerable to hypothermia. Adverse weather events – including heavy snowfall, high winds, landslides and floods – have led to Rothbury, at times, being cut off from the outside world; other than that, nothing else happens. Rural crime and incident demand is low, with the infrequent theft of metal, diesel and farm machinery, and the poaching of wildlife on outlying farms. Summer tourism heralded complaints of disorder by wild campers, off-road motorcycles, inconsiderate parking and speeding through villages. While rural crime and disorder may be low, such occurrences heighten people's fear of crime, especially in remote communities.

During my impromptu afternoon tea with my visiting colleagues, we discussed everything from force changes, officer misconduct, promotions, rural policing and, bizarrely, why I had one of the best sergeant jobs in the force. The conversation then returned to the purpose of their visit – the risk assessment for our newly recruited police volunteers, to enable them to open the police station for the public at weekends.

Following a brief visual inspection of the open-plan front office and visitor reception desk, my colleagues decided that a glass security screen was needed as a barrier between the public reception foyer and the working police office, to protect volunteers from harm.

'What? A great big bloody screen? Rothbury has never seen an angry man,' I retorted.

'Just in case,' came the reply. I shrugged my shoulders in bewilderment. We recruit police volunteers to work in the station to break down police–community barriers, only for the force to erect an internal security barrier to keep the volunteers at arm's length from the community who visit. The decision was not really a surprise – in fact, it was to be expected in a highly risk-averse organisation: 'Cover our backs, just in case anything were to happen.'

My colleagues said their goodbyes and left the station, refreshed and recuperated – no doubt swanning back to the 'demands' of the force training department. With peace and quiet in the office now restored, I took a moment to reflect: why was my neighbourhood sergeant role at Rothbury one of the best jobs in the force? Was it the personal responsibility and accountability given to me to oversee rural policing in Coquetdale, to reduce crime and build trust? Or the empowerment to develop relationships with organisations, such as the Northumberland National Park Authority, the Forestry Commission, the National Trust and other statutory and voluntary partners, working together to keep our rural communities safe?

Perhaps it was patrolling the picturesque, peaceful market

town of Rothbury, which straddles the River Coquet, meandering up the river valley through rolling hills, country estates and castles, stretching north to the border with Scotland? Or, maybe, it was the wonderful community I was proud to serve. Rothbury even has an unelected 'word-of-mouth' medieval council: the Four and Twenty Gentleman of Rothbury, headed by the vicar!

Perhaps it was a deep sense of personal pride, having been born and raised in a not too dissimilar mining community at Easington Colliery, County Durham, where people held the same values of respect, togetherness, resilience and compassion. Who knows? However, it was time to stop daydreaming and focus on police work – dusting down the annual summer policing plan to tackle tourism-related crime and disorder – speeding motorcycles, farm show events and the annual Rothbury Traditional Music Festival. Other than that, nothing much happens.

Rothbury Police Station is situated on the main street in the centre of the village, with the Coquetdale Arts Centre directly above, and the library next door. The premises are known locally as the Court Buildings; in the early sixties a magistrates' court, police station and stables were co-located there. The station is small but functional: a public reception area overlooks the front office, which has space for three computer desks, and leads to a rear room used for refreshments, locker storage and for speaking privately with visitors. A narrow passageway leads from the rear refreshment room to a hidden toilet, shared with art gallery staff and visitors.

As the Rothbury neighbourhood sergeant, I supervised a team of four police officers. Often we were like ships passing in the night, each working a different shift pattern, to cover the vast area of several hundred square miles of rural North Northumberland. Officers were accustomed to working in isolation, although police colleagues from Alnwick occasionally visited the station, as did the odd motor patrols officer or student police officer, calling in for a toilet stop during driver training around Northumberland and the Scottish borders.

Our neighbourhood police team had been highly innovative in our engagement with the community. Police and community priority-setting forums were introduced to empower the community to set their own priorities for the local police – usually speeding and parking. Rothbury established the first Northumbria Police support volunteer programme, with volunteer roles identified: to open the police station for the public; to attend parish council meetings; to provide visibility at farm show events; and to undertake community speed-watch deployments in villages where speeding was identified as a concern. Our newly recruited police volunteers served to strengthen police–community relations as positive advocates for the local policing team.

The introduction of community messaging at Rothbury was another first for the force. Each of the 16 parish councils were encouraged to sign up residents to receive police email updates and alerts. Hundreds of residents, businesses and local organisations joined community messaging. Obtaining the buy-in from the community, who became our eyes and ears, led to increased flows of community intelligence to support early police interventions to disrupt and deter crime. The mobile police station toured the area and local village surgeries were held, including 'Cuppa with a Copper', to improve police engagement with hard-to-reach rural communities. Several watch schemes were rolled out to reassure farm, church and caravan communities.

Partnership working was further strengthened by the establishment of a land-user group, which involved local police, Northumberland National Park Authority and other key organisations involved in land management. Joint patrols and rural crime operations were conducted in the early hours of the night. Neighbourhood officers built strong relationships with councillors, schools, doctors, businesses, volunteer groups and statutory bodies, including local authorities and health and education services. The words attributed to Sir Robert Peel, who founded the Metropolitan Police in 1829 – 'the public are the police and the police are the public' – best described the relationship between the police and the community.

Rothbury, which is actually a town the size of a large village, is located in North Northumberland, in North East England. The area forms part of the Alnwick Police sector. A prominent local landmark is the world-famous Alnwick Castle, a bastion of strength and resilience famously linked to the fictional wizard Harry Potter. Alnwick Police officers were led by the equally resilient Inspector Sue Peart, who had 'spellbinding' people skills, genuinely caring for her staff and the communities they served, especially Rothbury, where Sue lived.

Alnwick sector lies within the expansive Northumberland Area Command, with Berwick sector bordering Scotland to the north, Hexham to the west, and the former mining, industrial and port areas of Ashington, Bedlington and Blyth located to the south east. Chief Superintendent Mark Dennett, a highly experienced operational police commander, headed Northumberland Area Command.

In 2010 Northumbria Police, the sixth-largest police force in England and Wales, was led by Temporary Chief Constable

Sue Sim, the first female chief officer to do so. In addition to Northumberland, the force covered the heavily populated areas of Newcastle, Gateshead, North Tyneside, South Tyneside and Sunderland, situated 30 to 40 miles to the south, along the banks of the industrial rivers Tyne and Wear. Police resources were concentrated in those larger towns and cities – where demand was greater, and serious crime more prevalent – in contrast to rural North Northumberland.

Rothbury, known as the capital of Coquetdale, sits on the edge of Northumberland National Park. The area is one of the safest places to live in the UK, and is rarely touched by serious crime. Police radio circulations usually refer to missing people, or the occasional suspicious person or vehicle, often travelling north towards Scotland. Otherwise, there is a degree of autonomy in rural policing, detached from the crime and deprivation found in urban force areas.

SATURDAY, 3 JULY

One such police radio message was broadcast in the early hours of Saturday, 3 July 2010. The transmission related to a suspect male involved in a shooting incident which had taken place in Birtley, Gateshead, 40 miles south of Rothbury. The circumstances of the incident involved the man lying in wait outside his ex-girlfriend Samantha Stobbart's house. At 2:40 am Stobbart, together with her new partner, Chris Brown, left a neighbour's house and walked alongside the communal grass towards the front of her home. The suspect, armed with a double-barrelled sawn-off shotgun, confronted Chris Brown and, without compromise, blasted the gun at Brown, who staggered across the grass. A second shot was fired, seriously wounding Brown, and he fell to the ground. The suspect reloaded his gun and, at point-blank range, executed Chris Brown as he lay prone on the grass.

Screaming hysterically, Stobbart ran towards the safety of her home. The gunman followed. On seeing her through the front lounge window, he took aim and fired. Samantha Stobbart was seriously injured, suffering puncture wounds to her liver, pancreas and stomach. The offender ran from the scene. CCTV images captured him calmly walking along the road, where he flagged down a taxi.

The suspect was Raoul Thomas Moat.

Moat, 37, was by no means a prolific criminal offender. He was known to Northumbria Police and social services because of a history of domestic abuse with former partners. Intelligence suggested he was involved in enforcing retribution, linked to drugs. Moat had just been released from Durham Prison the previous Thursday, having served an 18-week prison sentence for assault on a child. Samantha Stobbart had been separated from Moat for over a year and had moved back in with her parents at Birtley. Moat's imprisonment had given her the opportunity to finally break free from his violent and coercive control. Stobbart then began a relationship with Chris Brown, a 29-year-old father of two, and in phone calls to the prison she made it clear to Moat that their relationship was over. She told him Brown was a karate instructor; he was younger, fitter and capable of looking after himself; and that he was a police officer (which was not true). To Moat, these words were incendiary.

While serving time in prison, Moat planned his revenge. He arranged for a sawn-off shotgun and cartridges to be procured by Karl Ness, his wood-cutting business partner. Ness also staked out the home of Stobbart to monitor her movements and liaisons with Brown. It later emerged that around the time of Moat's release from prison he changed his Facebook status, with the chilling words:

> Just got out of jail, I've lost everything, my business, my property and to top it all off, my lass has gone off with someone else … Watch and see what happens.

On Friday, the day after Moat's prison release, Ness delivered the gun and ammunition to his Newcastle home. Moat adapted the shotgun cartridges, loading them with lead fishing weights to increase their destructive effect. He was also seen visiting a nearby DIY store, where he purchased camping equipment. He was over six-feet tall, with short blond hair, and was wearing a distinctive orange T-shirt; the former club doorman had clearly maintained his strong muscular, body-building physique. The next day, Moat would use the shotgun to kill Chris Brown and seriously injure Samantha Stobbart.

Throughout the Saturday, detectives conducted urgent enquiries to locate Moat. His whereabouts, current associates and access to a vehicle were unknown. Specialist search teams supported by firearms units carried out address searches, including the search of Moat's home in the west end of Newcastle. Moat had installed CCTV, due to a deep mistrust of police, and during the house search numerous tape recordings of his conversations with social services were recovered. His mindset had clearly bordered on a state of paranoia.

Firearms officers initially entered the address to look for Moat, and in his absence they secured the house for the specialist search officers to painstakingly go through the property for evidence, room-by-room. The firearms officers were unexpectedly redeployed elsewhere, leaving the unarmed search team exposed. The search officers felt anxious and concerned for their safety, and representations were made to senior officers. The response was to 'just get on with it'. All the search officers completed police pocket notebook entries to document what they perceived as a total disregard for their safety.

As the search of Moat's home continued, the search officers, who worked in pairs, took refreshment breaks in their marked police personnel carriers parked outside the address. The officers were left in the dark as to any developments in the hunt for Moat, and so listened attentively to the local radio news bulletins on the vehicle's radio, where updates were more informative than internal police communications. Two officers found Moat's heavy chainsaw when searching the loft; he presumably used it for his log-cutting business. As a contingency, they planned to drop the chainsaw from the loft hatch onto Moat's head if he were to return to the address with a gun. Officers searching the surrounds of the house would duck behind Moat's trailer, which he used to carry logs, every time a car drove past the address. Between 10:00 pm and 11:00 pm, while on their break outside the address, officers noticed a dark saloon car loitering in the vicinity of the house. The vehicle left the area and the address search continued into the early hours of Sunday morning.

SUNDAY, 4 JULY

Shortly after midnight, Northumbria Police Communications received a 999 emergency call:

Hello there, this is the gunmen from Birtley last night, my name is Raoul Moat…

My girlfriend has been having an affair behind my back with one of your officers, this gentleman I shot last night, the karate instructor. You have been on to me for years. You have hassled us and harassed us, you just won't leave us alone … if he hadn't been a police officer, I wouldn't have shot him … I didn't mean to shoot her like that, right. He deserved it …

But the fact of the matter is, I am not coming in alive … come anywhere near me and I will kill yous. I've got two hostages at the minute, right. Come anywhere near me and I will kill them as well. I am coming to get yous, I am not on the run, I am coming to get you. I have lost everything through yous. You killed me and him before the trigger was ever pulled … You will get your chance to kill us right, you will get your chance to kill us. You want me to kill myself but I am gonna give you a chance because I am hunting for officers now.

Moat's emotive voice showed a clear determination of intent, hell-bent on revenge against police officers who he had a deep hatred towards. Chris Brown was dead, but he was not a police officer and never had been. The 999 call to Northumbria Police was immediately referred to the Duty Silver Commander, Superintendent Jo Farrell, to assess the seriousness of the threat and determine actions to protect the public and police officers.

At around the same time, 00:20 am, Police Constable David Rathband parked his motor patrols vehicle on the tarmac verge of the flyover roundabout above the A1, at the intersection with the A69 – a main arterial route to Newcastle and Gateshead. The traffic officer was single-crewed and nearing the end of his late-day tour of duty. While sat in the driver's seat, he observed vehicles negotiating the roundabout from this highly visible static point, which was well-lit during the hours of darkness.

Meanwhile, Moat and his business partner Karl Ness, 26, were being driven around Newcastle in a black Lexus saloon by mechanic Qhuram Awan, 23. Police were not aware Raoul Moat was travelling in his mate's Lexus, and 12 minutes after his 999 call to Northumbria Police Moat spotted PC Rathband parked up in his marked police vehicle. Moat got out of the Lexus and approached the front passenger side of the patrol car, armed with the sawn-off shotgun. As PC Rathband turned towards him, Moat, without any emotion, blasted the gun through the vehicle's side window.

PC Rathband suffered gunshot wounds to his face and fell sideways across the front seats. Moat, at point-blank range, discharged a further shot to the officer's head. PC Rathband was seriously injured, and fearing there was worse to come he played dead. Moat ran from the scene and made off in the black Lexus, together with Awan and Ness. Despite his injuries, the officer managed to reach for his police radio to alert police communications staff that he had been shot. David Rathband, a 42-year-old married father of two, had suffered the most appalling, life-threatening head injuries.

Listening to police radio transmissions at the time were the unarmed search officers still inside Moat's house, less than two miles from the roundabout scene. Without hesitation, the sergeant directed his search team to abandon the house.

'Get out now,' he shouted. Search equipment was left in situ as the officers bolted from the address. Police personnel carriers were driven out of the street at speed, heading for the security of their base at Newcastle North Police Station. Armed police were deployed to the station entrance and the public front office was closed: the building was placed in lockdown. Police officers and staff were moved to the secure custody suite at the rear of the station complex for their safety. How ironic that the custody suite was commandeered to protect unarmed officers, police staff and prisoners.

The search officers, while catching their breath at the station, were astonished to discover that Moat was a passenger in a black Lexus car, similar in appearance to the black saloon car they had seen loitering outside his house during the property search. With PC Rathband in a critical condition, subsequent information confirmed the black saloon car was the same Lexus vehicle. The search officers were extremely relieved to learn that Moat had decided there were too many police outside his house to take them all out; 'There but for the grace of God, go I.'

PC Rathband had suffered life-threatening head and facial injuries and was rushed to Newcastle General Hospital by ambulance, under police escort. T/Chief Constable Sue Sim attended the hospital together with PC Rathband's wife, Kath, while he had emergency surgery to try to save his life and his sight. The officer showed immense courage to pull through, later describing the incident:

> The big flash from the gun lit up the whole of my face. The noise was like my head inside a can. It was worse, just the noise. I knew I was in trouble the amount of blood I was losing. I just knew I was going to bleed to death.[1]

PC Rathband didn't regain his sight and was never able to

---

1 David Rathband, speaking in 'Real Crime: Raoul Moat Part 2'. (28 Nov 2011). Available from https://www.youtube.com/watch?v=jKR3FZED1V0 [Accessed 1 Nov 2019]

see his wife and children again. The incident would have a profound effect on the officer, his family and his life.

Within an hour of the incident, Moat contacted Northumbria Police:

> Hello, this is Raoul, the Birtley gunman. Are you taking me serious now? I've just downed your officer at the roundabout in the west end of Newcastle. Yeah, well I'm gonna destroy a few lives like you destroyed mine. This is what happens when you push, push and push. I tell you now, I'm absolutely not going to stop. You're going to have to kill me cos I am never going to stop.

The shooting of PC David Rathband was a significant escalation, from the domestic revenge killing of Christopher Brown to the attempted murder of an unarmed police officer, by a gunman with a determination to hunt and kill others. Moat's declaration that he had two hostages brought a further public safety dynamic to police tactics, even though police considered the revelation dubious. In addition to safeguarding the public and the welfare of potential hostages, the leadership of Northumbria Police were faced with a dilemma. How do you protect a predominantly unarmed police force from a gunman on the run, intent on indiscriminately hunting down and killing officers? This was probably one of the few times in a police officer's career where the gravity of the situation bonded all officers of all ranks together with a shared fear, and unified their determination to resolve the incident.

Unarmed front-line officers expected senior police leadership to afford them protection, given their impotence in facing an armed and dangerous criminal. Bewilderingly, Northumbria Police, despite all its force planning, firearms training and critical incident management, never had a contingency in place to deal with an armed gunman, despite the fact that, four weeks prior (in the neighbouring force area of Cumbria), gunman Derrick Bird had gone on a rampage, shooting 12 members of the public dead.

Following the attempted murder of PC Rathband, and a clear statement of intent by Moat to kill officers, the police investigation was conducted at a pace throughout the Sunday. Enquiries included: address searches by firearms teams; the arrest of suspected associates; the use of informants, surveillance, telecom data; and public press appeals for information. Force intelligence officers, detectives, specialist crime units and uniform resources worked flat out to try to make a positive breakthrough. And always at the back of their minds was the question: who next?

Northumbria Police implemented a revised patrol strategy because of the high threat level to police officers. At 9:00 pm on Sunday evening, senior management briefed all officers on duty across the force. Elements of the patrol strategy included:

- All uniformed resources double-crewed. No foot patrols.
- Incidents graded as urgent or high priority to be attended by two police vehicles.
- No resources to remain in static positions when on patrol.
- Armed response vehicles to operate across the force at all times.
- All incident logs potentially linked to Moat to be switched to Silver Command (senior officer).
- Sightings of Moat to be referred to the Tactical Firearms Commander.

- A recognised phrase to be transmitted where an immediate threat has been identified relating to Moat attacking a police officer, with all unarmed officers to return to police premises immediately, using blue lights and sirens.

Security at police premises was stepped up with increased staff vigilance. Firearms officers were deployed to protect Newcastle North Police Station and Northumbria Police Headquarters, based at Ponteland on the outskirts of Newcastle. Officers were also directed not to travel to work in 'half-blues' (wearing police uniform under a civilian coat.)

At Rothbury, policing throughout the Sunday evening continued as normal. The lone patrol officer, PC Gresswell, was assigned to attend minor road traffic collisions, alarm activations and trees obstructing roads due to the high winds. A female Rothbury resident who reported a previous relationship with Moat volunteered to hand personal letters to police at the station on Monday morning.

At 10:30 pm, PC Gresswell was allocated a high-priority domestic incident at Harbottle, Northumberland, a remote rural village, nine miles north-west of Rothbury. The officer felt a deep sense of unease in attending high-priority incidents single-crewed in the absence of another officer to double-up with. After he dealt with the domestic dispute, PC Gresswell left Harbottle to drive back to Rothbury. During the journey he was contacted on his police radio by a rather irate Alnwick Police sergeant, who queried why he had attended the incident single-crewed and not complied with the new patrol policy. PC Gresswell was stunned. No one had bothered to communicate a revised patrol strategy to him, nor had anyone informed the control room radio dispatcher, hence his attendance at several incidents single-crewed, which left him isolated and vulnerable.

The officer felt compromised and immediately returned to Rothbury in the darkness of night, with the wind bellowing, trees rustling and streets empty. The police station on the main street appeared desolate. A tense PC Gresswell abandoned his police vehicle at the front of the station. Whether through fear, intuition or imagination, the officer sensed someone was watching him: a shadow in the dark alleyway to the side of the police building. The alley, which was eerily pitch black, led to the unlit rear of the station, where there were insecure and dilapidated former police stables. Without hesitation, an anxious PC Gresswell entered the police office, discarded the police car keys, collected his coat and immediately terminated duty. The officer then drove his own car 12 miles across the moors to the sanctuary of Alnwick Police Station to liaise with concerned colleagues.

The ripple effect that followed the random, merciless shooting of PC David Rathband and the manhunt for Raoul Moat touched all operational officers across the force.

A heightened state of alertness brought a nervous sense of realisation: the most dangerous people are those who have nothing to lose.

MONDAY, 5 JULY

The identity of the black Lexus IS 200 SE saloon car, registration V322 HKX, used by Moat and his associates, was confirmed in video footage from PC Rathband's patrol car. Investigating officers were convinced that Ness and Awan were not hostages, but the imprecise nature of the situation introduced a level of caution. A 49-page letter, written by Moat and delivered to a friend's address, was recovered by police. The contents appeared to be a long-winded justification for his actions, and they gave an insight into the motivation behind his threats to kill police: 'They hunted me for years, now it's my turn.' Events took a further unexpected turn when a handwritten letter from one of the 'hostages' was posted to a family member and handed over to police. The letter reinforced police misgivings:

BURN THIS LETTER!!!

DEAR …

IT IS MY FRIEND THAT HIS HOLDING ME 'HOSTAGE'

I AM SAFER THAN SAFE. BUT THIS DEED WILL SEE ME A MADE MAN.

IM ACTUALLY HIDDEN OUT AT A SECRET LOCATION WELL OUT OF HARMS WAY.

BURN THIS LETTER AFTER YOU HAVE READ IT. NOT SURE ABOUT SHOWING IT TO MAM AND DAD THOUGH AS THEY WILL SPILL THE BEANS AND THAT WILL LEAD ME TO ACTUALLY BEING SHOT.

LOVE YOU XXX

BURN THIS LETTER!!!

Interest from both local and national news organisations intensified, ratcheting up the pressure on senior officers as police issued a series of public appeals for information. Details of the black Lexus were released, and the public were warned not to approach it. Police confirmed Samantha Stobbart was no longer in a critical condition and Northumbria Police issued a plea to Moat on her behalf: 'Please give yourself up. If you still loved me and our baby you would not be doing this.' Detective Chief Superintendent Neil Adamson, the senior officer in charge of the investigation, also made a direct appeal: 'Mr Moat, I have made a number of requests to you to contact police and hand yourself in. That opportunity still exists.'

Northumbria Police revealed that the force had been warned by Durham Prison the previous Friday that Moat may intend to cause serious harm to his partner. Police were unable to comment further as the case had been referred to the Independent Police Complaints Commission (IPCC).

At 10:25 pm on the Monday evening, a robbery was reported at a fish takeaway shop at Seaton Delaval, a former mining village in South East Northumberland, ten miles east of Newcastle. A male matching the description of Raoul Moat and in possession of a sawn-off shotgun entered the fish shop and demanded cash. As officers travelled to the scene, the force helicopter, call sign I99, was airborne in the vicinity, deployed to a missing-person search. The I99 crew, believing the suspect to be Moat, made a request to the force control room to pull out of the missing-person search and divert to the robbery. Control room supervision refused permission. Police enquiries at the scene revealed the robbery suspect was Moat. An area search was conducted but found no trace of the offender or vehicle.

Under agreed mutual-aid arrangements, specialist armed resources travelled to Northumbria Police from several police forces, including Cumbria, Cleveland, Humberside and South Yorkshire Police. Additional firearms support officers arrived from the larger metropolitan forces of West Yorkshire Police and the Metropolitan Police, totalling some 160 officers. Northumbria Police circulated safety advice to all officers:

> Moat is highly emotional, armed and extremely dangerous. He has made specific threats to harm police officers and staff. No firearms have been recovered. Should the vehicle be sighted, do not under any circumstances approach.

As Monday drew to a close, nearly three days had passed since Moat had begun his murderous retribution. Communities across the North East felt edgy, with Northumbria Police unable to take control and having to react to events, with an unrelenting Moat clearly in the driver's seat. Unarmed police officers were tense and fearful that the force was unable to protect them from an armed gunman. The decision of whether to expediently train and issue firearms to uniform patrol officers for protection did not appear to be an option senior police officers would actively contemplate, nor have the will to implement.

TUESDAY, 6 JULY

Leaving home at 7:00 am on Tuesday morning to drive to Rothbury for early day duty, I reflected on the day in hand. While aware of the developing Moat situation and the danger posed to police following the incidents in Birtley and Newcastle, I had no immediate concerns of events directly impacting on remote, rural Rothbury. As I travelled north up the A1 towards Alnwick, the day was as pleasant as any other July morning – the early sun was rising through cloudless blue skies, the scenic Northumberland countryside wore its array of summer greenery and distant fields of golden wheat were readying for harvest. A beautiful day was in store.

I was intending to head west along the Coquet Valley to Rothbury, when my mobile phone unexpectedly rang. It was Inspector Sue Peart, who sounded uneasy. Without the customary pleasantries she said, 'Graham, do not under any circumstances go to Rothbury – head straight to Alnwick and I will see you there.'

Sensing a three-line whip in the urgency and tone of her direction, I confirmed I understood. The call was abruptly terminated. Intuitively, I felt the instruction pointed towards Moat's presence in the Rothbury area. I had an instant adrenaline rush in anticipation of some major development in the hunt for him. I began to speculate, with a sense of alarm, about the risk to my colleagues and the vulnerability of my Rothbury community.

I entered Alnwick, a traditional Northumberland market town, and drove straight to Alnwick Police Station, arriving at 7:40 am. I walked through to the parade room on the ground floor where a police dog handler, typing away at a computer, casually uttered, 'He's at Rothbury.' I nodded in acknowledgement, my thoughts confirmed, and headed upstairs to the inspector's office for the 8:00 am morning meeting. Inspector Sue Peart was in her office – welcoming, caring and professional as always, but with a seriousness in her presence. We awaited the arrival of the Alnwick Neighbourhood Sergeant Neville Wharrier, the 24/7 response sergeant and Alnwick intelligence officer.

Sue confirmed, in confidence, that Moat's black Lexus had been found that morning at Rothbury industrial estate, unaware that early day officers in the parade room already had this information from the night shift dog handler. Control room supervision had not formally told the inspector of the vehicle's sighting; ironically, a member of the public had phoned Alnwick

Police earlier, wanting to speak to the plain-clothes officer who was at the industrial estate to ask if it was Moat's car that had been found. One sensed that the sector had been temporarily bypassed as irrelevant to the situation in hand.

In Rothbury, the black Lexus was parked unattended at the far end of the small industrial estate, in a cul-de-sac adjacent to several micro-business units. The riverbank was nearby, alongside an old railway track bed that led away from the industrial estate and cut through the hillside, surrounded by farmland. A dog walker had found the car shortly before 7:00 am and contacted police. All available firearms officers had been dispatched to the location to secure the scene and find Moat.

I was mindful of the Rothbury community. The small businesses on the industrial estate were due to open at 8:00 am, and parents and children would soon be leaving home to walk to the nearby school. Local people and visitors would be enjoying an early-morning summer stroll along the riverbank and old railway path. Worryingly, word-of-mouth in a close-knit rural village travels faster than social media, and can quickly spread fear and apprehension.

As dawn was breaking, Rothbury was slowly wakening to an armed gunman at large in the village, with an intention to kill. Nothing ever happens in Rothbury – until now.

2
TRANQUILLITY
TO TURMOIL

The Alnwick morning meeting, in many respects, was routine: a review of incidents, crimes, intelligence, safeguarding and resources. Rothbury was the exception. Local policing was, in effect, suspended as firearms officers rushed to the village to find Moat and his 'hostage' associates. As the meeting concluded, there was a collective feeling of nervous excitement – a renewed sense of purpose and anticipation – as updates from firearms officers were eagerly awaited.

Sergeant Wharrier and I were tasked with monitoring Rothbury incident activity from the safety and comfort of Alnwick neighbourhood police office. A reassurance incident log was created in anticipation of capturing community information concerning Moat. In such situations, where there is a potential for multiple incident creations due to numerous calls from the public, the main working incident will be deemed the parent log, and all other related incidents cross-referenced as child logs to effectively manage incident demand.

There was only one incident of note: the initial sighting of the black Lexus at Rothbury industrial estate, as reported by the dog walker. A local building company, based on the industrial estate, had also contacted police after they noticed the suspicious vehicle while opening up their premises. From intelligence sources, it was apparent that police were already aware of the approximate location of the black Lexus at 10:00 pm the previous night.

With the vehicle found, and the occupants presumed to be in proximity, there was a disagreement between two senior police officers over tactics to locate and detain Moat. A specialist crime superintendent wanted the Lexus recovered for forensics, and the immediate location to be staked out by covertly armed undercover police officers. An operations superintendent disagreed; the safety of the public was a priority, and visibly armed police must be deployed to contain the area and apprehend Moat.

Logically, once the public were aware of Moat's Lexus parked on the industrial estate, fears would escalate, and deploying concealed armed officers, lying in wait, would not serve to dispel those anxieties. In the absence of any visible police presence to reassure and protect the community, local residents, including the many shotgun-owning farmers, may well have put their guns at the ready to protect themselves. Senior police commanders asserted that the priority must be public safety and reassurance, and so armed response officers, both uniform and plain clothes, flooded into Rothbury to secure the immediate area of the industrial estate in search of Moat.

Before long, residents were phoning neighbourhood officers to enquire if the rumours about Moat being in the village were true. In observing developments at a distance, from the neighbourhood office at Alnwick some 12 miles away, I could feel the tension in the air: the emotion in calls from concerned members of the public; edgy radio transmissions from officers arriving at the scene; and the tentative incident updates, as if an armed showdown between Moat and police was imminent.

At 9:45 am force Communications made an urgent request for local Alnwick officers to identify a rendezvous point (RVP) for armed officers travelling to Rothbury. I suggested Debden car park, an enclosed woodland parking area one mile outside of the village, opposite Cragside House on the B6341 eastern approach into Rothbury. Cragside House, gardens and estate is a well-known tourist landmark owned by the National Trust.

Several minutes later, at 10:00 am, a 'burglary dwelling' (a domestic burglary) was reported at a bungalow in the area of Walby Hill, Rothbury. The female caller stated that while she was in the shower someone had entered her home through a ground-floor bedroom window at the side of her house. Items had been disturbed in the bedroom and food taken from the fridge. The bungalow was situated just off the main road into the village. Across the road from the house was the entrance to Riverside. Riverside comprises a row of large houses facing towards a public footpath, and a scenic grassed area which sits adjacent to the river. A series of cylindrical stepping stones led across the river from Riverside towards the entrance to Roth-bury industrial estate – literally a stone's throw away from where Moat's vehicle was found abandoned.

The police radio dispatcher allocated me and my Rothbury colleague PC Trevor Weldon to travel the 12 miles from Aln-wick to attend the burglary. My initial reaction was concern. The incident, in my view, was clearly linked to Moat so I requested armed response officers (already deployed in the vicinity) to attend the scene in the first instance, to carry out an investiga-tive assessment. I appended an update on the burglary incident log to outline my rationale – burglary dwellings in Rothbury were extremely rare; the incident will be linked to armed suspect Raoul Moat.

Burglary dwellings in Rothbury and Coquetdale are uncommon – there are maybe two or three per year. Such reports generally involve entry and theft from the garage adjoining the side of a residential house, as opposed to entry to the house via a window or door. Non-residential burglaries were also infrequent; there are around 20 crimes per year – often when entry has been gained to a shed, workshop, barn or other outbuilding. The reported burglary dwelling at Walby Hill referred to entry via a ground-floor bedroom window, which was highly unusual itself as well as being in the area where Moat was believed to be present.

The radio dispatch operator switched the incident to the operations room, for review by senior officers overseeing firearms deployments to Rothbury. The Operational Support Commander decided local unarmed officers must attend as initially directed. There was no rationale for this direction updated on the incident log nor, I suggest, is it likely to have been documented elsewhere. The decision did not appear to give much weight to local officer knowledge, or ensure the right resource attended the right incident at the right time: armed officers to conduct an initial investigative assessment. I acknowledge police officers are not averse to risk, but neither are they impervious to harm. In light of the shooting of PC Rathband, the decision appeared ill-judged or worse, reckless. There was clearly a raised threat to unarmed officers in attending the incident, but they were sent regardless. Having worked in a critical incident management environment, I am acutely aware of senior officer decisions made in the safety of far-distant control room 'bunkers', detached from the realities of policing on the coalface.

PC Trevor Weldon and I put on our protective vests and tooled up with our police batons and CS incapacitant spray. We found a marked police van in the rear police station yard and made our way towards Alnwick Moor and Rothbury. In a disciplined organisation, no matter how inept you feel leadership decisions are, you just have to get on with it and hope for the best.

Around the time we set off from Alnwick, a Forestry Commission employee working in the area of Cragside Estate, Rothbury, drove his vehicle into Debden car park. He noticed armed police officers in civilian clothes parked up in several unmarked cars. The forestry ranger asked the officers what they were up to. 'It's just an exercise,' they told him. He acknowledged their explanation, although he remained unconvinced, and then headed down towards Rothbury, where he turned left along the B6344 road that runs alongside the river, away from Rothbury, towards Forestry Commission workshops situated on the edge of Cragside Estate.

As the forestry ranger drove along the winding riverside road, bordered by trees and farmland, he noticed two men in front of him, walking one behind the other on the left side of the road, heading away from Rothbury. Both men were in their mid-20s: one was of large build, six-feet tall, white, unshaven and had receding hair; the other was a similar build, of Asian appearance, and was unshaven with short dark hair. Forestry Commission staff work closely with local police, keeping a watchful eye on happenings across the estate. The vigilant and intuitive ranger immediately turned his vehicle around and sped back to Debden car park. He approached the same armed officers and disclosed the information concerning the two men, in support of their 'exercise'. The officers decamped at break-neck speed en masse, driving from the car park in the direction of where the two men had been sighted.

The force helicopter was swiftly above the location, hovering over the two suspects, who were visible beneath the overhanging trees of Cragside Estate as they walked along the riverside road. The helicopter camera downloaded live footage to police commanders in the operations room as firearms units travelled to the area. The first unmarked armed response car approached the men from the direction they were heading towards. Officers confirmed their sighting to colleagues following behind, and three unmarked police vehicles screeched to a halt alongside the men, boxing them in as stun grenades were launched, exploding like firecrackers at their feet. The suspects instinctively dropped to the ground. It was all over in ten seconds. Both were securely detained, handcuffed without resistance and identified as Karl Ness and Qhuram Awan; clearly they were no longer deemed to be hostages.

The situation had been fast moving, with police radio transmissions in overdrive. Officers showed an excitable willingness to get involved, although a more measured approach may have been desirable, especially with an armed and hostile Moat still in the immediate area. At the time of the arrests, PC Weldon and I were three miles outside of Rothbury, travelling down towards Cragside, en route to the Walby Hill burglary. A police radio call requested two police vans attend Cragend Farm to collect the two prisoners. We diverted to Cragend Farm, a cluster of farm buildings just off the riverside road near where the two men had been arrested. Another police van was travelling across from Alnwick, and I asked the radio operator if the principal

[Moat] was one of those arrested. 'No' was the response. The force appeared to throw caution to the wind; ourselves, and other unarmed colleagues in prisoner vans, were directed to the location, to run the gauntlet of an armed gunman still at large in the immediate area, and hunting police.

As we drove past the main entrance to Cragside on our left, with Debden car park opposite, the force helicopter was hovering overhead, the loud, incessant whirling of its blades disturbing the woodland tranquillity. While listening to police radio transmissions, I was made aware of concerns for the safety of 15 walkers stranded in Debden carpark. A motor patrols officer was tasked with attending, but by sheer coincidence a local ambulance paramedic drove into the car park, noticed the group and told the walkers they needed to leave the area immediately. He was aware of Moat's presence in Rothbury following a visit from armed police officers an hour earlier, enquiring as to why he had driven his ambulance along the industrial estate at 7:30 am that morning. The walkers had just been dropped off and their bus had left the car park minutes earlier. The paramedic, in his 4x4 ambulance utility vehicle, drove out of the car park, chased after the bus, stopped it on the moors and asked the driver to return and collect the walking party. The motor patrols officer arrived at the car park as the walkers were being ushered onto the bus to be driven away from the area, out of harm's way.

Travelling at speed along the riverside road, PC Weldon and I then turned off after a mile and drove along a short entrance track to Cragend Farm. I noticed several marked and unmarked armed response vehicles parked on the square gravel courtyard enclosed by a farmhouse and stone farm buildings. Armed officers from South Yorkshire Police had the two male suspects detained and handcuffed. The second police van arrived soon afterwards and Alnwick officers placed Qhuram Awan inside the caged cell in the rear of their vehicle. A clear plastic bag containing property was handed over by a South Yorkshire officer, who confirmed the property was Awan's, seized on arrest. I approached Karl Ness, the other suspect, who was handcuffed to his rear. The arresting officer handed the prisoner over to me and I asked if there was any property with the prisoner, to which the response was no. Ness was escorted to the police van and put inside the secure prisoner cell at the rear of our vehicle. He was compliant, although he avoided conversation, and appeared somewhat dishevelled. He was heavily built, overweight, sweating and, to put it bluntly, shitting himself.

Force Communications directed we take Ness to Newcastle North custody suite some 30 miles away, and Awan to Middle Engine Lane, North Tyneside. PC Weldon drove the prisoner van from Cragend Farm. Ness remained passive and appeared deep in thought. During the journey I received a phone call from a detective sergeant who was overseeing the CID officers awaiting our arrival in custody. 'Did Ness have any mobile phones when arrested?' he said. I told him that there was no property in his possession, unlike Awan, who had property seized. After a couple of minutes the same detective rang back to clarify once more. I explained that I had specifically asked the South Yorkshire officer on prisoner transfer and they had clearly stated that Ness had no property.

An element of doubt entered my thoughts. Was Ness actually searched by firearms officers on arrest? You would expect so – for weapons, guns, phones or other evidence; however, an elementary principle of policing is to never assume. In view of the question raised by the detective sergeant, and my growing misgivings, I directed PC Weldon to pull the police van off the A697 into a secluded lay-by hidden by trees, to revisit the search of Ness. I opened the rear prisoner cell door and asked Ness if he had any mobile phones on him. 'Yes,' he replied. I informed Ness that he would be searched, and, with police batons and CS gas at hand, I warned him that any obstructive thoughts, or a bid to escape, would be unwise. Ness was polite and fully cooperated in the recovery of two mobile phones from his jacket pockets. I informed a relieved detective sergeant, who notified the CID team at Newcastle North custody suite. On reflection, when the handover of Ness took place, from firearms officers to PC Weldon and me, the question I should have asked was, 'Has Ness been searched?' as opposed to, 'Has Ness any property?' It's a subtle but significant difference in questioning, and a searching error on my part. We all live and learn!

As we travelled south down the A1 towards Newcastle, I noticed at least 15 unmarked cars, presumably specialist operations, speeding north towards Rothbury. With their sirens blazing and magnetic roof lights flashing, I remember thinking, 'I hope they all have maps'. Throughout the journey, Ness appeared quiet and anxious, evident by his stillness and the sweating on his brow, but he remained civil at all times. We arrived at Newcastle North Police Station at 11:25 am, where the circumstances were outlined to the custody sergeant, the seized phones handed over to CID officers and police witness statements completed.

In Rothbury, a two-mile ground exclusion zone had been set up around the village, with police urging residents to stay indoors. Armed police officers manned checkpoints and all vehicles entering the exclusion zone were searched; no vehicles were allowed to leave. Waves of firearms officers were deployed to locate Moat and protect the community. The slow pace of rural life abruptly gave way under the presence of heavily armed, paramilitary-style police officers converging on the defenceless village as the hunt for Moat intensified.

Northumbria Police issued a press update on Cragend Farm. The force revealed there had been a potential hostage situation and the two men involved were arrested on conspiracy to commit murder. A Northumberland County Council helpline was introduced to provide support to the people of Rothbury, and neighbourhood police officers and police volunteers were tasked with telephoning and reassuring all of our community contacts and concerned residents.

At 12:30 pm, PC Weldon and I left Newcastle North custody suite to return to Alnwick. We anxiously awaited updates from Rothbury on any positive sightings of Moat, or his capture, although, information was vague. During the journey we were diverted to Longhorsley St Helens C of E First School, to set up a reception centre for displaced children and parents. Longhorsley, a quaint rural village, with a church, pub and post office, nestles just off the main A697 arterial road nine miles south of Rothbury.

The plan was for armed police to escort Rothbury schoolchildren living in remote outer village areas from Dr Thomlinson C of E Middle School at Rothbury to the reception centre at Longhorsley, to be reunited with their parents. Conversely, students who attended King Edward VI High School in Morpeth, a town eight miles away, would rendezvous with police at the reception centre and their bus would be escorted back to Rothbury.

On arrival at Longhorsley First School I was greeted by the

headteacher and her staff, who were so supportive and willing to do whatever was needed to accommodate police, parents and children. From a police perspective, my priority was to put in place systems to manage the flow of pupils and parents; record all attendees; ensure effective external communications; and secure the use of a quiet room for anyone vulnerable or in need of support.

A Northumbria Police media statement and community message update was released to Rothbury residents:

> This is an update in relation to the search currently ongoing in the Rothbury area, for Raoul Thomas Moat, who at this stage has not been found. The two-mile radial exclusion zone on the ground remains, as does the air exclusion zone. Police continue to advise the public to stay indoors as a precautionary measure and await further instructions. We have armed police officers on the streets who are there to protect and reassure the public. There is no need for alarm.
>
> We are working closely with the local authority and are advising parents that children at school in Rothbury will be kept at school at the moment, where they will be looked after by teaching staff. We are seeking the cooperation of parents and residents during this time, as no one will be allowed in or out of Rothbury until further notice.
>
> A reception centre has been set up at Longhorsley First School, where local authority staff, police officers and health staff will provide support to anyone returning to Rothbury who is unable to do so. Alternatively, people should make alternative arrangements to stay with friends or relatives outside the Rothbury area. These are precautionary measures while police searches are underway. We thank the public for their cooperation during this challenging time.

Following the departure of Longhorsley schoolchildren at the end of lessons, I awaited the arrival of residents, parents and pupils in transit from Rothbury and Morpeth. In the calmness of the near-empty school building, I noticed the TV on the wall, broadcasting the latest national news headlines: 'Hunt for Raoul Moat' – 'Gunman on the Run' – 'Rothbury Residents in Fear'. At that point I realised the enormity of the situation unfolding and the huge national media interest. It suddenly dawned on me that I had better reply to my partner Jan's earlier text, enquiring whether I was okay.

With the focus and intensity of work I became somewhat oblivious to the feelings of family at home. I contacted Jan to reassure her and, to my surprise, found she was more up to date with events than I was. That morning she had been at a friend's house for coffee, together with other parents of young children. One of the mothers, Kate, the wife of a serving Newcastle-based police officer, mentioned Moat during conversation and Jan intimated that I would be alright up at Rothbury. She returned home around lunchtime and put the radio on, unaware of Moat's presence in Rothbury. Hearing the intense media coverage and watching the live television broadcasts of the ongoing manhunt centred on Rothbury, her legs suddenly turned to jelly.

In the afternoon, Jan received a further call from Kate asking if she was okay, elderly neighbours from across the road called at the door, and friends and family members sent texts offering support. How touching it is to know there is a great unconditional strength of love from family, friends and neighbours that comes together when there is a perceived sense of need or wellbeing, not just in policing, but in other public, emergency and armed services. We really owe an immense debt of gratitude.

Back at the reception centre, the anticipated flow of children and parents failed to materialise. Rothbury schoolchildren were escorted out of the village by bus and dropped off near their homes. Likewise, the high school students from Morpeth were transported directly to Rothbury, accompanied by police, to be reunited with parents. Only two Morpeth students and one Rothbury pupil attended the reception centre to await collection by their parents. There were no further reception centre requirements as school transit arrangements for the following days were yet to be decided.

Northumberland Area Commander, Chief Superintendent Mark Dennett, attended Longhorsley First School and met with local TV reporters. The senior officer gave the first of many television interviews to inform and reassure the local community. The warmth and trust in the relationship between Northumbria Police and the local media was evident, as was the slick media operation, with his press interview shown soon afterwards, during the 6:00 pm local television news bulletin.

With the reception centre stood down, I returned to Alnwick Police Station around 7:00 pm. A major manhunt for Raoul Moat – Operation Bulwark – was in full swing and Rothbury remained in lockdown, with armed police checkpoints in position. All people and vehicles entering the two-mile exclusion zone were searched. Elizabeth Clifton, an eighty-five-year-old resident and police volunteer, summed up the resilience of local people. While returning home, driving the small red car she had named 'Fizzy', Elizabeth was stopped at a police checkpoint and her car was searched:

'The police officers were ever so polite,' she said. 'But I told them I had served during the war and defeated Hitler – I am not in the slightest scared of that bugger!'

The community, while anxious and somewhat bewildered, were reassured by the presence of armed police officers, noticeable on almost every street corner. They were also intrigued by the mass of media reporters and camera crews descending on the village. As darkness fell, the streets were visibly devoid of people, who had retreated to the sanctuary of their homes. With nightfall, came an impasse – the sound of silence. Moat had gone to ground with nowhere to run, but many places to hide.

At 10:00 pm I set off for home reflecting: 'What a day!' The early-morning sun rising through clear blue skies, and the scenic countryside and fields of wheat, were all now distant memories, as the manhunt for Raoul Moat focused the eyes of the world on a peaceful Northumberland village; tranquillity at dawn, turmoil at dusk.

3
MANHUNT

Overnight searches for Moat were unproductive. The Northumberland countryside presented many challenges; it's a mosaic of ancient meadows, hills, forests, river valleys, heather landscape and dense undergrowth. Police had already discovered his makeshift campsite on grassland near Wagtail Farm, close to the old railway cutting that led from the industrial estate. Police dogs were sent in first to search the tent, which appeared to have been abandoned along with a duvet, sleeping bag and camping gear. The dogs were up for the task, tearing the tent apart and dismantling the deserted campsite in a matter of seconds, but Moat had fled. Armed officers and the force helicopter searched the immediate area without success.

Amongst the contents discarded in the tent, police found an eight-page personal letter addressed to Samantha Stobbart, in which Moat attempted to justify his actions, and a hit list of social workers and police officers who he believed had wronged him. A dictaphone was also recovered, which contained rambling recordings of his thoughts and his utter contempt of the media for the perceived lies published about his character, family background and previous relationships. Moat clearly had the means to listen to media broadcasts and, enraged, he'd recorded these words:

> The next lie I see in the paper, I'm going to kill an innocent member of the public.

His volatile state of mind in making a direct threat to kill the public would significantly escalate the challenge for police in protecting the Rothbury community.

The lack of a force contingency in planning for a gunman who threatened to shoot police and the public came to bear. Police were on the back foot, having to react to rapidly changing events as dictated by Moat. Firearms resources were significantly increased and additional armed response vehicles and sniper-trained officers were seconded from external police forces, through mutual aid. Specialist armed forces personnel were also reported to have been deployed.

Several concerned residents reported the streets of Rothbury empty of visible armed police officers in the early morning from 5:00 am, as if they had all gone home, only to return at 8:00 am to resume day shift patrols. Police officers who lived in the village felt particularly anxious due to the threat to their safety and the perception that Rothbury had been left unprotected. Measures were taken to ensure an armed response presence was visible in the village centre at all times.

Police search teams, supported by firearms officers, conducted systematic searches in the area of Moat's abandoned tent. The search of wild vegetation, moorland, farmland, forestry and riverbanks was exceptionally demanding. The threat of stumbling across a gunman in hiding, willing to pull the trigger on any officer discovering his lair, was real. Northumberland National

Park Authority and Mountain Rescue Team volunteers provided expertise and local knowledge of the terrain and rural landscape to assist senior police commanders in the search.

At the outset, police motivation and morale was strong. Officers were aware of the danger to themselves and colleagues; nonetheless, each had determination and pride in their police role to see this through – to protect the public and bring Moat to justice. Despite the lack of force planning and preparation for such an unprecedented, dynamic situation, there was an expectation that the collective strength and resolve of the force would prevail. Police leadership had to adapt and think on their feet, although shortcomings soon became apparent.

Police command involved a Gold, Silver and Bronze structure: Gold (chief officer), decided the overall strategy or game plan to be accomplished; Silver (senior officer), determined the tactical objectives to achieve the Gold strategy; and Bronze leadership, at operational level, oversaw resources to carry out the objectives set by Silver. Problems emerged with the blurring of Gold and Silver Command roles, as Gold chief officers attended Silver Command briefings, influencing Silver tactical decision-making. The Tactical Firearms Commander (Silver) was unable to effectively oversee the many simultaneous firearms operations and deployments. This was resolved, following a suggestion from a seconded West Yorkshire superintendent, by appointing several Tactical Firearms Commanders, each overseeing separate firearms deployments.

The RVP for firearms and search teams was at the Rothbury industrial estate, the area where Moat's Lexus was found abandoned. With raised riverbanks, heavy undergrowth and thicket surrounding the location, officers believed the area was not secure; they were sitting ducks if Moat wanted to ambush or take aim. All searches were coordinated from an operations room based at force headquarters; search teams received a map with a zone, which they would mark with a double cross when searched. However, zones that had been searched were not securely contained, so Moat could re-enter unhindered and go into hiding.

Communications between police commanders, specialist fire-arms officers and search teams were at times unclear. Unarmed search officers were directed by Silver Command to search a field, just outside the village. On arrival, they came across a plain-clothes Metropolitan Police officer, parked up in an unmarked car at the field entrance. The officer warned them not to go into the field as there were armed camouflaged officers concealed there. 'You will get shot,' he said. The search officers immediately left the area, bemused at the poor communications that could have compromised their safety.

Speculation had been mounting that Moat may have hidden in a drainage culvert, which diverts flood water into the river. The outlet is on Riverside, just along the public footpath from the stepping stones. Bizarrely, the force control room had received a call from a lady in South Africa, professing to be a psychic, who stated that the suspect was hiding in a storm drain. Armed police, equipped with ballistic shields, opened the heavy metal entrance gate and searched the culvert. There was no trace of Moat or evidence of disturbance in ground silt that would have indicated someone had been there.

A local static caravan site that adjoined the industrial estate was not searched within the first two days of Moat's arrival in Rothbury, and site residents expressed concern. Officers on the ground felt the planning and coordination of local searches, at times, were found wanting. In fairness, the force obtained specialist search advice at a national level. The expansive rural village landscape and outdoor nooks and crannies would have presented challenges for any police force or military organisation.

RAF Tornado jets equipped with thermal imaging were deployed. Repeat reconnaissance photographs were taken and examined for signs of recent disturbance in the terrain. A fixed-wing aircraft from Greater Manchester Police had apparently been put on standby to attend, although Northumbria Police Air Support Unit officers, who operate the force helicopter, did not feel a fixed-wing aircraft was required. One of the civilian aircraft observers got the impression that either senior police leaders did not fully understand the full capabilities of the helicopter or were overly guarded as to what hidden detail or covert operations the crew may have got wind of.

During the hours of darkness before the early sunrise, a planned tactic for any sightings or intelligence on the whereabouts of Moat was to deploy the police helicopter at low level. The aircraft's high-intensity light beam would be used to illuminate the location, disorientate Moat and seek to flush him out.

Intelligence was received that Moat might have been hiding in a camouflaged shelter. The informant, who was in prison at the time, was authorised by prison authorities to travel to Rothbury under armed police protection. The decision to use the prisoner to identify the concealed location of an armed Moat was of high risk to the individual. Further intelligence also revealed that Moat might have been in possession of homemade explosives. The hidden bolthole was found, but there was nothing to suggest Moat had been there.

Under intense pressure, Northumbria Police brought in TV expert bush tracker Ray Mears. Officers were impressed with his techniques, which culminated in search dogs, armed with the smell of Moat's scent, finding some disturbance in vegetation which was attributed to Moat. It remains questionable as to whether Mears was ever close to locating Moat, contrary to his subsequent claims, which appeared to coincide with the launch of a book.

Police made numerous arrests and rounded up anyone suspected of assisting Moat. Press appeals sought further information on his whereabouts and to establish if there were any links with people living in Rothbury. Information from specialist police intelligence operatives was obtained but not always shared with the local force intelligence officers. 'Going straight to the top,' a frustrated colleague said.

The sheer volume of information received from the public, and generated internally within Northumbria Police, overwhelmed force intelligence officers. All items of information and intelligence needed to be evaluated in relation to its source, reliability and content, and the handling of intelligence, determining links with other information and dissemination to officers all required consideration. Northumbria Police had no system in place capable of managing the vast quantity of information and intelligence.

In serious crimes such as homicide, police forces across the UK use HOLMES 2 (Home Office Large Major Enquiry System) to process the mass of information and ensure no vital clues are overlooked, improving the effectiveness of the investigation. There was no such comparable IT system in England and Wales to support police forces in managing the avalanche of information from major or critical incidents, such as Moat, despite it being one of the main recommendations of the Bichard Inquiry, published in 2004, following the murder of two schoolgirls in Soham, Cambridgeshire, in 2002:

> A national IT system for England and Wales to support police intelligence should be introduced as a matter of urgency.
>
> —*Recommendation 1, Bichard Inquiry, 2004*

Some forces had implemented their own ad hoc information handling systems to try to bridge the gap. This suggestion was made by an officer from Humberside Police, who was seconded to Northumbria Police at the time; however, it was deemed not practicable to implement. Without effective IT systems to sift through the sheer volume of information to determine relevance – such as reported sightings, shadows and rather vague calls of the 'I dreamt I saw Moat' variety – the task was rather hopeless. It was akin to sorting out confetti into petals of substance and trying to link them to hundreds of other petals that were possibly connected. With no such systems, the manual handling of the vast amount of information and intelligence – generated by police, public and media – was all over the place.

Media interest reached saturation point as the world's TV and press landed on Rothbury. Live 24/7 news coverage shaped public perceptions, and the intensity of the media interest was a concern to senior officers as it began to adversely impact on the investigation. Relationships between Northumbria Police and the local media were strong, with well-established mutual trust. However, several national media organisations adopted an imposing, aggressive, agenda-setting approach. Their destructive dissection of Moat's character and previous relationships led to Moat threatening to kill a member of the public for every piece of inaccurate information published. The people of Rothbury were yet to be told of this.

Senior police officers pleaded with the press to tone down damaging content as it was fanning the flames of a volatile Moat. Some media organisations believed their own hierarchy of needs took primacy over the police priorities of protecting the community and conducting a murder investigation. To countenance the destructive reporting of Moat, the press gave prominence to the sympathetic views of his brother, Angus Moat. Media coverage swiftly turned into a family soap opera, which distracted from the need to locate Moat and prevent harm to the people of Rothbury.

Police offered a £10,000 reward for information leading to the direct capture of Raoul Moat. In an attempt to pacify the media, Northumbria Police allowed them access to officers conducting searches near Beggars Rigg car park, situated just outside the village. The attending press were led to believe the search was real; however, the event was apparently staged for the media. Police officers involved were utterly dismayed and felt the performance needlessly detracted valuable police resources from the priority of finding Moat. More so, it appeared to demonstrate that Northumbria Police leadership and the force media department – some 40 staff – lacked the expertise and experience in handling the media at this pressurised level.

Developing professional working relationships with both the print and broadcast media to support the investigation and reassure communities was a challenge for any senior police officer. The force media department attempted to strike an almost impossible balance; to feed the press appetite for newsworthy material while being ever mindful not to get sucked into a rampant media agenda for instant news and sensationalised content. As the insatiable demands of the media began to run riot, negative media reports and personal attacks on the chief constable became a significant distraction for senior investigating officers. This was a relationship that was hard to live with, in a situation where neither was able to live without the other.

Meanwhile, Northumbria Police officers and staff at every level, without exception, worked relentlessly with sheer determination to protect the community and bring the situation to an end. The public response to police information requests was amazing, with endless reports of suspicious males, premises entered, allotments disturbed and suspect sightings; the community were so resilient. As every day passed, it became clear that the people of Rothbury would hold the key to resolving this manhunt. In support of the neighbourhood police team, police support volunteers, led by local coordinator David Brown, MBE, a highly respected former Police Authority member, telephoned over 200 residents to provide reassurance.

Numerous reports of sightings were made in and around Rothbury: at Thrum Mill, Garleigh Road, Jubilee Crescent, Simonside, Whiton Bank, Wagtail Road, Reaver's Well, Hepple, Cragside and Northumberland Council Depot on Riverside. Armed response officers attended a report of two suspicious males in the remote Northumberland village of Elsdon – two men were arrested. Information was received of a man hiding in undergrowth along the B6344 riverside road. The man was located by the force helicopter and challenged on the ground by armed officers. He didn't move, and police feared the man was dead, but suddenly he awakened. He turned out to be a local drunk who was a little dazed at having his sleep abruptly disturbed, but was otherwise fine.

Several reports were received of properties disturbed, including a burglary at Rothbury Football Club, not far from where Ness and Awan had been detained. Local police officers were also tasked to attend a nearby stables around midday, to follow up a report that the premises had been found insecure.

Firearms officers had previously attended the same stables after an earlier report of a suspicious male, but the search by armed officers was negative and the stable buildings had been resecured. Several horses were escorted by firearms officers to the top field, away from the riverbank. On the opposite side of the river stood Wagtail Farm, the area where Moat's tent was discovered. Horse riders would regularly cross the shallow water to exercise their animals and ride along the bridleways near the farm.

The frightened female informant stated that the stable was now insecure again, with the entrance door ajar and fresh footprints found in the mud nearby. PC Dave Brown and PC Roxy Bird attended the incident in a marked police vehicle – a Ford Connect known as a 'Noddy' van. The local officers, unarmed, drove along the uneven, sloping track to the isolated cluster of stables which were surrounded by rolling green pastures where the horses grazed. After speaking to the informant, the officers trod cautiously while conducting a cursory check of the stable buildings. An anxious PC Brown had his Taser at the ready as a last means of protection, although it would be no match for Moat, armed as he was with a sawn-off shotgun.

As they quietly tiptoed along a path heading away from the

stables, they noticed one of the windows of a static caravan was smashed. The damage appeared recent, with fragments of broken glass scattered on the ground. In the sudden belief they had discovered Moat's hideout, and fearing for their lives, they turned and ran. The officers scrambled into their police vehicle and hastily drove away from the stables. Back at the station, both officers were relieved, but furious at having been placed in such a high-risk, dangerous situation.

Dave and Roxy, both personal friends, felt they had been put in a perilous position that seriously compromised their safety. PC Brown drew parallels with his Royal Military Police service in Berlin, where the IRA paramilitary organisation targeted the armed forces, except that he had a side firearm in Berlin. PC Brown submitted a critical report to the chief inspector, making representations that he and his colleague, both unarmed, were unnecessarily placed in danger at an incident and location where Moat's presence could reasonably be foreseen. Also of note is that there were firearms officers nearby and available for deployment. At the time of writing, PC Brown is still awaiting a reply.

While further searches of the area failed to find Moat, colleagues of the officers highlighted similar situations. Local unarmed officers were directed by the control room to follow up incidents or make enquiries in areas in close proximity to the gunman. It begs the question why unarmed police officers were put in such positions when the risk was obvious and real, bearing in mind the recent cold-blooded shooting of PC Rathband.

Incidents such as sightings were initially risk-assessed by senior officers in the Gold room to determine the threat level to the public and police. Armed response officers were deployed to those incidents where the threat level was deemed high, or, when information on incidents was imprecise, to conduct what is known as an investigative assessment. Where a search for Moat by firearms officers was unsuccessful, the incident would be either finalised or delayed, usually for reallocation to local officers. Follow-up enquiries were likely to include contact with the informant, scene enquiries, a victim statement, a report of crime or other investigative actions.

The force recognised and sought to address the danger to unarmed officers, and to afford some protection to local police undertaking high-visibility patrols. Northumbria Police obtained around 20 ballistic-protected police vehicles from the Police Service of Northern Ireland. The armoured vehicles were a vast improvement for officer safety; however, unarmed officers were still vulnerable when leaving their vehicles in order to conduct enquiries. Directing local officers to check unsecured buildings or re-attend incidents originally reported as suspicious (in respect of Moat), raised serious questions: had the threat that required the initial deployment of armed officers significantly diminished to the level where local unarmed officers could safely conduct enquiries, in an area where Moat was still believed to be at large? The deep-rooted organisational pigeonholing of police resources into specific areas of work may provide an explanation of the reluctance to re-allocate armed response officers to follow up enquiries that, ordinarily, uniform cops would deal with, even though the threat from an armed gunman in the area was still evident and real.

The potential threat to Roxy and Dave was either ignored or unduly diminished, with the leadership mindset being that all police officers are not averse to risk and have enhanced personal protective equipment. But those leaders were not driving police Noddy vans to suspicious incidents in an area where a gunman was at large. There appeared to be a disconnect between the distant hierarchical management of such incidents, with the officers deployed on the front line, clearly placing them in harm's way, to the detriment of officer morale, trust and confidence.

There was also a disconnect between the various police resources – neighbourhood, firearms, CID, search teams, specialist operations and intelligence – working in Rothbury. All officers and police staff worked diligently and professionally within their own vertical leadership silos. There was, however, little contact horizontally, other than the occasional exchange of pleasantries. This detached approach can present communication issues, leading to unnecessary duplication, or it can compromise officer safety (as evident in the field search), with the left hand not knowing what the right hand is doing. A solution, as in any major incident, would have been to establish a forward control point to enable local supervision on the ground to communicate, share information and local knowledge.

Another area of concern was the disjointed incident handling at the Communications department, based at force headquarters on the outskirts of Newcastle. Call handlers would receive information from the public, and create new computer incident logs, or update information on numerous existing incidents. Entries on incident logs were also appended by Communications supervision, operational support staff, the enquiries desk and senior officers, including critical incident directions and authorisations.

The incident logs would then be switched to the radio dispatch operators' queue, and stack up for their attention. The

Rothbury radio dispatchers were expected to review numerous computer logs, find the relevant log entry and action the update, as well as oversee radio communications and requests from officers deployed on the ground. It was a case of too many hands on too many incidents, leading to the saturation and overload of radio dispatchers. At times, information was overlooked and real-time decisions were delayed and actions not taken.

While the sheer hard work and determination of communications staff was exceptional, an examination of incident logs throughout the Moat period highlighted flaws in command and control. As the situation developed in Rothbury, the lack of a bespoke Silver Command room to manage critical operational decisions was evident. A Gold Command room stood in its place, where those tactical operational decisions were made; however, the function of Gold is to support the chief officer at a strategic level, as opposed to becoming entwined in Silver tactical decision-making responsibilities, which should be kept separate.

Furthermore, officers working in the Gold Command room were in a separate room to Communications supervision and their radio dispatch operators. This resulted in numerous incidents being switched between radio dispatchers, Communications supervision and Gold room senior commanders, which affected dynamic incident command and control. There appeared to be little detail of decision-making ownership by a named senior officer in the Gold room on incident logs. Furthermore, there was negligible buy-in of local policing knowledge, which was not sought or given prominence, as if local officers were superfluous to the 'superior' know-how of Gold room command.

The volume of calls to police, and the reporting of incidents linked to Moat, was overwhelming. The force was restricted in its ability to process the material. Multiple incident logs were in existence, with endless pages of log entries, which inevitably led to information being overlooked. Officers who were normally based in force headquarters' departments were wheeled out of their day-to-day desk jobs. They were tasked with sifting through the countless pages of incident logs to review the information, ensure actions had been taken, update callers, and provide reassurance – thus duplicating the work Alnwick officers and staff were already undertaking.

With no breakthrough in the hunt for Moat, the community, and an increasingly hostile media, were becoming more anxious. There was growing criticism, and doubts as to the capability of the force in bringing the incident to a positive conclusion. Despite this, local neighbourhood police officers were determined to maintain a visible presence in the village. Officers carried out reassurance patrols, attended incidents and engaged with the community, despite concerns for their personal safety.

In his role of Bronze Commander, overseeing community resilience, Chief Superintendent Mark Dennett had his ear firmly to the ground. As Northumberland Area Commander, Mr Dennett was respected by most, and avoided by a few who had unwisely crossed his rank. His operational background and experience, especially in critical incidents and firearms, was solid and he understood the concerns and frustrations of his locally deployed officers, drawn from across Northumberland Area Command. In response to officer criticism and a sense of disillusionment, Chief Superintendent Dennett sent an email to all Area Command officers. He stated, that in times of difficulty, he reverted to the words of Theodore Roosevelt. [2]

> It is not the critic who counts, nor the man who points out how the strong man stumbles, or where the doer of deeds could have done better. The credit belongs to the man who is actually in the arena, whose face is marred by dust and sweat and blood [...] who knows the great enthusiasms, the great devotions [...] who at best knows, in the end, the triumph of high achievement and who, at the worst, if he fails, at least he fails while daring greatly, so that his place shall never be with those cold and timid souls who know neither victory nor defeat.

The effect of the email was to calm anxieties, lessen the criticism toward others and refocus officers on their role – to safeguard and reassure the public – with an appreciation that everyone in the force was working together to bring the incident to a close. The communication from Chief Superintendent Dennett, while no doubt reflectional, was a highly effective leadership response to reset the tone and motivation of all officers under his command. In truth, the content was more akin to war and did not reflect the genuine safety fears of his officers. If the correspondence had been sent by a less-experienced or less-respected senior officer, its interpretation would have leant more towards 'management bullshit'.

Rothbury officers, together with visiting colleagues from other police sectors, were encouraged in their community role. Northumberland Chief Inspector Mick Todd (a tall, commanding, old-fashioned copper), Alnwick Inspector Sue Peart,

---

2   'The Man in the Arena' is a passage from the 'Citizenship in a Republic' speech by Theodore Roosevelt, given at The Sorbonne, Paris, April 1910

Alnwick Neighbourhood Sergeant Neville Wharrier, and I, were ever-present in Rothbury – engaging with the officers, holding parade briefings, conducting end-of-shift debriefs and actively undertaking uniform patrols.

Our neighbourhood police officers could not have been more dedicated. PC Trevor Weldon voluntarily returned home early from his family caravan holiday down south to give his all to the cause. High-visibility patrols were conducted in Rothbury and the surrounding areas at all times of the day. Key community groups, partners and volunteer organisations were personally updated by neighbourhood officers. Police support volunteers contacted elderly and concerned residents to provide some comfort, and community message updates were sent to hundreds of residents and businesses on an almost daily basis. Old-fashioned but highly effective 'A' boards were placed at prominent locations on the High Street, displaying the latest information for people passing by.

Despite the many challenges faced by police officers during what was a dynamic, imprecise and unprecedented incident, their sheer professionalism and determination would always overcome any bumps in the road to bring the situation to an end. Although the manhunt was intense and worrying, the strength and togetherness of the community was unwavering. Relationships and trust in Northumbria Police were built on strong foundations.

The quote, attributed to Sir Robert Peel, 'the police are the public and the public are the police', while true, could also mirror the families of police officers: so far from the nature of policing, yet so close, to understand and feel the emotional strain at the end of each working day. The constant stream of media headlines and live feeds from Rothbury allowed police families to relate directly to an otherwise opaque policing role, giving them a shared, if indirect, understanding and involvement.

PC Lawrie Ward, who was based at Rothbury, worked tirelessly each day for his community. At the end of each tour of duty, Lawrie would arrive home in the late evening, where the sound of his young son could be heard shouting, from his darkened bedroom, 'Dad, Dad!' Lawrie checked on his son as any father would do. His son inquisitively asked, with excited expectation, 'Have you got him yet, Dad, have you got him?' Lawrie would reply, 'No, not yet, son. Time for bed now.'

As another day drew to a close, the resilience of residents and the commitment of police to find fugitive Moat remained steadfast; however, there were visible signs of fatigue. His whereabouts was still unknown, with no confirmed sightings, as if he had simply disappeared without trace. It was a manhunt losing momentum; a community showing signs of despair; a police force under strain; a village still under siege.

4
VILLAGE
UNDER SIEGE

As I lay in bed in the early hours of Thursday morning, I kept thinking, 'How is this all going to end?' There were no meaningful developments in the hunt for Moat, and community concerns were escalating, influenced by the world's media who had descended en masse with little sensitivity for the feelings of residents. There were relentless live broadcasts and dramatic news headlines as well as so-called expert analysis and growing criticism undermining Northumbria Police. At times this was personally directed at T/Chief Constable Sue Sim. Police officers and staff at every rank and in every role worked all hours, day and night, to keep the people of Rothbury safe and bring this incident to a close.

My thoughts were, that in any given situation there would be a tipping point where either there was a significant breakthrough or, conversely, the community, fuelled by a rampant media, would turn against the mass intrusion, and desperation would give way to anger and resentment. I reflected on the successful handling of previous major incidents in Rothbury, such as floods and a serious gas supply disruption in winter. In any major incident, whatever the scale, the way to take the community with you is to engage from the outset: with the right people, at the right time, through the right medium, to achieve the right effect.

The four-day gas disruption in early February 2009 was a case in point. The incident left many elderly and vulnerable residents at risk of hypothermia, and neighbourhood officers went straight in: working with partners to protect residents; providing community updates; conducting high-visibility patrols; and supporting the setting up of a reception centre at the Rothbury Jubilee Hall. The start of the Moat incident was similar: community message updates, enhanced policing presence, and the establishment of a reception centre at Longhorsley First School.

During the gas incident, Chief Fire Officer Brian Hesler (who lived in the village) and I immediately formed a local resilience forum, and key partners who worked in the community were invited to attend. Local representations included Northumberland County Council (fire, highways and adult services), the NHS (mental health, ambulance), councillors, and leaders of several voluntary organisations. The forum prioritised community reassurance and the identification and protection of people at risk. Continuous engagement with the public helped shape the partnership response to meet the needs of residents. The outcome was a return to normality with no casualties and a stronger cohesive community. A similar resilience forum was implemented in response to the river flooding, where we worked with partners and the community to overcome the challenges together.

Rather bizarrely, in learning from those incidents, my philosophy on developing partnership engagement took the form of a 'tree-top' analogy. Most community organisations in our towns and villages can be notionally depicted as trees of differing sizes. The branches reflect the people within each organisation and the communities they serve. Rothbury Neighbourhood Policing Team focused on building relationships with the 'tree tops' of those organisations, thus connecting with their branches of people. The branches included statutory partners (namely, local authorities, health services and schools), non-statutory partners (such as parish and county councillors, national parks and forestry), and voluntary organisations (business forums, resident associations and charities).

Furthermore, the introduction of community messaging improved communication with those organisations, their staff and the wider community. Watch schemes were also expanded to strengthen links with the many farming, church and caravan communities. In achieving buy-in from the vast majority of people, Rothbury and Coquetdale became a stronger, cohesive and more resilient community, better prepared to face future challenges and threats together.

With no indication of a breakthrough in the hunt for Moat, and signs of growing community frustration, I felt there was a need to replicate the neighbourhood policing of the previous major incidents at Rothbury by reaching out directly to those key partner organisations and residents and listening and responding to their concerns. The significant investment already made in building those relationships would bear fruit in times of need, and the time had come.

After a sleepless night, and with the dawn chorus in full voice, I set off for the morning meeting in Alnwick. The nightmare scenario of losing the confidence of the Rothbury community was forgotten, replaced by a renewed determination to persuade Northumbria Police to go with a key partnership resilience forum, and a public meeting to listen to, understand, and address the needs of the community.

When I arrived at Alnwick Police Office there was little in the way of positive news overnight as the manhunt at Rothbury entered its third day. At the morning meeting, attended by Chief Inspector Mick Todd, Inspector Sue Peart, Sergeant Neville Wharrier and me, all were receptive to my proposal for a meeting of key partners and a community public forum. The decision, however, sat with senior Bronze and Silver commanders, so it was a case of awaiting a response for the go-ahead.

Sunny weather served to dispel some of the gloom clouding the village, as rays of village life prevailed. Children attended school accompanied closely by parents, and residents visited the bank and high street shops with defiant smiles and a shrug of the shoulders. The presence of armed police conducting foot patrols in a quaint Northumberland village was a sight to behold. Officers were dressed in black paramilitary-style uniforms, carried assault rifles, and wore ballistic helmets which resembled those worn by German soldiers in World War II. Armed police mingled with children and grannies, which appeared rather surreal in a village that was supposedly 'under siege', and where residents had been advised to stay indoors. Police officers, including our armed 'boys with toys', while consummately professional, were only human; they had families, grandparents and children of their own. All were directed to adopt a 'neighbourhood policing style', which I believe meant smile and speak to the public. I would expect this in most given situations. Our dear Rothbury resident Elizabeth Clifton was flabbergasted:

> I saw a mother and two young children outside the police station, who seemed a little anxious on seeing police in uniform, wearing helmets and carrying guns. Another policeman got out of the dog van, produced two hand puppets from the glove box, and entertained them. It was marvellous.

I hoped Elizabeth, on seeing armed police officers wearing ballistic helmets that resembled those of German soldiers, would not antagonise them, having fought off Hitler during the war! She continued:

> I then bumped into Sue [Inspector Sue Peart] who introduced me to Chief Superintendent Dennett, who spoke with me for ten minutes. I cannot believe he would take the time to talk to little old me.

Elizabeth reflected the resilience of the people of Rothbury: so proud of their community, so respectful of their police.

As I drove into Rothbury later that morning, I couldn't help but notice the saturation of media vehicles, satellite communication vans, press pitches and live news updates from nationally recognised presenters. Television producers, camera crews, sound engineers and print journalists milled around, basking in the glorious sunshine. Every common area of grass had been requisitioned by some press organisation or other to cover an event played out live on TV and radio, and online. While local business and high street trade was at a standstill, hoteliers and guest house proprietors were buoyant. There wasn't a vacancy in sight because of the media influx.

Rothbury Police Station bustled with uniformed police officers; colleagues called at the station to use the single communal toilet, have refreshments, or use one of the two computers in the small front office. Proportionate to its size, the station was by far the busiest in the force. Surprisingly, there were no armed police protecting the building, which was situated on the main street. Nearby were alleyways and paths that ran 100 yards or so down to the river. The lack of armed officers to protect the station was possibly a senior officer oversight. The status of Rothbury Police Office was not in any way comparable to Northumbria Police's HQ or Newcastle North Area Command, although the threat to officers was arguably greater in a building highly exposed to the armed presence of Moat, especially in the dead of night.

While at the station, I was made aware that Silver Command had authorised a police meeting with key partners, and an evening public forum. I immediately set out to inform local partners that the meeting was to be held at 3:30 pm at the nearby Jubilee Hall. By virtue of our already well-connected relationships, Rothbury Reassurance and Resilience Forum was arranged and ready to go within three hours of being authorised. There was a clear purpose: to listen to, understand and provide reassurance about the concerns of our local partners. Senior police leaders deemed the forum to be a Critical Independent Advisory Group (IAG), which appeared to reflect the terminology in some strategic document. A rather vague IAG panel was apparently in existence at Berwick, some 40 miles to the north, to cover any major occurrence in North Northumberland; however, it was too far removed from Rothbury to have any material effect.

The public meeting for the Rothbury community was arranged for 6:30 pm, also at the Jubilee Hall, which was centrally located in the village. I liaised with the force media department to arrange a press release, notify the community and invite their attendance. Farm Watch circulations, community message bulletins and 'A' board updates on the High Street, also gave notice:

Northumbria Police Press Information – 13:30 hrs 08/07/10:

The searches in this area have proved a particular challenge due to the open farmland and dense woodland ...

Our enquiries have so far led to two men [Ness and Awan] being charged in connection with the investigation, and who will appear at court this morning. We continue to seek help from the public ... please call straight away.

Northumbria Police invite you to attend a community forum tonight: 6.30 pm at the Jubilee Hall Rothbury where local and senior officers will be present ...

While I prepared for both meetings, Rothbury neighbourhood colleagues continued with the agreed patrol strategy: visibility at key locations, visits to schools, and leaflet drops to vulnerable and elderly residents (with support from neighbourhood wardens). Local officers dealt with reported incidents, contacted callers, updated reassurance logs and reviewed community impact assessments with supervision.

Search teams and firearms officers painstakingly carried out their arduous, never-ending searches. CID officers charged Ness and Awan with conspiracy to commit murder and firearms-related offences; both appeared at court and were remanded to prison. A press appeal from Moat's uncle pleaded for his nephew to give himself up; however, he remained elusive.

At 3.00 pm I left Rothbury Police Office and walked down the High Street towards the Jubilee Hall, which sits on the corner of Bridge Street (which leads across the river to the industrial estate, middle school and community hospital). En route I met Inspector Sue Peart, who was accompanied by Chief Superintendent Mark Dennett, who was to chair the meeting in his capacity as Bronze Commander (reassurance). The Jubilee Institute meeting venue has been at the heart of the Rothbury community since 1897; it has several meeting rooms and a main hall used for dances, theatre shows and local events.

As attendees arrived for the partnership meeting, the tone was friendly but purposeful as you would expect. I counted 35 people present, with representatives from the various branches of the community: doctors, headteachers, local authority representatives, emergency services, parish councillors, publicans, businesses, land-user organisations and volunteer groups. It was pretty remarkable that so many key people from the community attended within three hours of being notified, which was a measure of their concerns.

Before the meeting, senior investigation officers released information to the media, disclosing that there was now a threat to the public from Moat. The communication, to some extent, appeared to have blindsided Chief Superintendent Dennett. An armed gunman who was now threatening the public was a significant change in the magnitude of threat. The information would severely affect community fear, and it created a greater need for public protection and reassurance. Senior investigation officers appeared to have been working within the confines of their investigation silo, with less-than-effective internal communications or consideration given to colleagues responsible for overseeing community safety and reassurance.

Police partnership meetings tend to follow a similar path – the chair provides an update, reinforces key messages and responds to any questions, or defers if unable to provide an answer. Mr Dennett opened the meeting with the latest police update, key reassurance messages and clarified some areas of concern. Listening attentively was Heather Cape, head teacher of Dr Thomlinson C of E Middle School. Heather asked a question which was so cutting in its simplicity, meaning and accountability – 'What does this mean for me?' – referring to the threat to her school, with over 200 children, situated just up the hill from Rothbury industrial estate. Should she keep the school open? What should she do to ensure the safety of her children?

Chief Superintendent Dennett wisely refrained from the usual stock answer that any decision was a matter for the school. In a measured way he acknowledged the question, and without directly responding to address her concerns he deferred the answer to buy time and determine a response with chief officers. A corporate response would clearly not have sufficed for the headteacher or, indeed, any person in the room. They were all now faced with a real threat from a gunman – who had already killed – on the run in their community. What did it mean for the people of Rothbury?

With less than two hours to go before the public forum was due to take place, the spotlight was on Northumbria Police to provide answers. The partnership meeting concluded around 5:00 pm, with the closing words from Alnwick Inspector Sue Peart – an impassioned rallying call, which lifted the spirit and the belief of everyone in the room. The meeting was well-received, positive and productive, with an agreement to reconvene at 11:00 am on Saturday, 10 July. Afterwards, Inspector Peart and I discussed arrangements for the Rothbury public forum. Chief

Superintendent Dennett liaised with senior colleagues and read a prepared media statement to television broadcasters:

> We still believe Mr Moat's main grievances are against the police; however, more recent information received indicates Mr Moat may pose a threat to the wider public. There is a heightened risk, but nothing to suggest Mr Moat is intending to target a specific part of the community. Our message is to go about your business as usual but be vigilant. If you see anything suspicious or out of the ordinary, report it to police immediately by dialling 999.
>
> The safety of the public has always been our number one priority. There are an extremely large number of armed and unarmed officers on the streets to protect and reassure the public. We still believe Mr Moat to be in the Rothbury area, although enquiries are ongoing throughout the force area. We have received overwhelming support from the community here in Rothbury, and from colleagues across the country, as well as specialist advice from a number of different agencies. Our intention remains to apprehend Raoul Moat safely and bring this to an end.

This carefully crafted press statement was clearly constructed to inform the public of the raised threat in a low-key way, undoubtedly with the aim of negating any escalating fears or community tension; a poetic interpretation perhaps, of the actual words understood to have been said by Moat:

> The next lie I see in the paper, I'm going to kill an innocent member of the public.

At 6:00 pm I returned to the Jubilee Institute in eager anticipation of the community forum that was due to start at 6:30 pm. Several media organisations and residents began to gather in the main hall, which had a seating capacity of 250. The hall was a traditional rectangular dance hall, with high ceilings, draped window curtains and a performance stage. As more and more people of all ages arrived, the younger children were requested to relinquish their seats and sit on the raised stage at the front of the hall, directly behind the seats reserved for the senior police panel. Concerns were expressed at the presence of the media, who had assembled camera tripods down the central aisle between the rows of chairs. Northumbria Police press officers allowed the members of the media to remain to record and photograph, but not to ask questions. They were moved to the sides and rear of the hall.

With the Rothbury community still streaming into the hall, senior officers took to their seats, including Chief Superintendent Mark Dennett, Northumberland Chief Fire Officer Brian Hesler and T/Chief Constable Sue Sim. The hall was packed to the rafters, with every seat occupied. People sat on the floor in the central aisle or stood jam-packed at the back of the hall, and around 20 children, who looked rather bemused, perched on the stage behind the assembled panel. The lady responsible for hall bookings appeared rather nervous at more than 400 people being crammed into a hall with a capacity of 250. 'Not to worry,' I thought. The chief constable and chief fire officer were on the panel, so if anything were to go wrong I was sure she would defer to them as being responsible for holding the event.

T/Chief Constable Sue Sim was no stranger to Rothbury. She had previously attended a community priority-setting forum in the same hall, following an invite from police volunteer coordinator David Brown, who was also a former Northumbria Police Authority member. Inspector Sue Peart also had a good personal relationship with Mrs Sim, having previously worked with the chief as her staff officer. Having received a friendly welcome, T/Chief Constable Sim thanked the residents for their attendance and, to lighten the mood, mimicked an air stewardess when signposting the hall's emergency exits, which went down well.

Mrs Sim addressed the raised threat posed by Moat to the people of Rothbury. She stated, 'There is an increasing position where we think he may be more of a threat to the wider community, that is anywhere.'

The chief constable stressed that there was no specific threat to the Rothbury community. Her friendly and approachable manner towards the audience shone through, easing any public anxieties. I did wonder at the time if the actual threat from Moat was greater than the impression she gave. I do not in any way believe there was an intention to mislead the public, but more an inclination to reduce fear and reassure her community. As with the earlier media release, comforting reassuring public statements are fine and only scrutinised later if events turn out to the contrary.

After her opening address, Mrs Sim responded to public concerns about the safety and vulnerability of schoolchildren by agreeing to post firearms officers permanently at the school to protect children and calm the fears of parents. Further audience questions sought clarification as to whether the Rothbury Traditional Music Festival would still go ahead in ten days' time, which was clearly in doubt. The mood of the forum lightened when children on the stage started to ask fairly articulate questions of the chief constable, text-messaged to them by family members seated in the audience.

A final question came from a resident: 'Are you finished?

Because I want to get home for my tea!' The community forum ended in laughter and people left the hall heartened and appreciative of the time taken by police to listen and provide answers to their concerns. Mrs Sim had been warmly received and applauded, gaining much respect. After the event, an elderly male approached her and said, 'Don't worry.' Mrs Sim told him that she *did* worry about her communities. The gentleman replied, 'Don't worry, we've all got guns under the bed.' Both had a chuckle, which summed up the warmth and spirit between police and the community.

I returned to the station, where on the top of my in-tray were several letters and cards. One card was addressed to 'All the police force' and read:

> To everyone that's trying to get this nutter off the streets. We would like to say thank you very much for putting your lives in danger to save ours.

The card was signed by two young children. It gave a sense of how an incident of this magnitude affected all residents, young and old.

There was no further information on the whereabouts of Raoul Moat. Public calls to the police continued unabated, with numerous reported sightings in and around the village. Firearms officers responded, but there was still no trace of the fugitive. Around midnight, police received a report of a suspicious male in the allotments, which were located just up the hill from the entrance to Riverside, next to the recreation club car park. The caller, a retired police officer, reported the male trespassing in the allotments, where he scrambled towards a shed. The readily available source of food in an allotment, and the reliability of the informant, raised the hopes of the deployed firearms officers. The site was searched without success. Further sightings were reported overnight, including a suspicious motor vehicle in the area of Riverside. The car was checked out by armed officers, but nothing untoward was found.

FRIDAY, 9 JULY

On Friday morning, an incident was reported to police by a female resident. The lady had noticed a suspicious male walking near her home on Riverside at around 10:30 pm the previous night, shortly before the report of the suspect male at the nearby allotments. She described the man as being of large build, dressed in black with a hood up, and wearing a baseball cap. The caller did not contact police at the time; however, after she discussed the incident with a builder who visited her house on the Friday morning, she decided it would be best to inform police before setting out to work. An incident log was created and put on delay; local uniform officers would contact the caller on her return from work later that day.

In Rothbury the media were still camped out, enjoying the scenic rural setting. Local Berwick MP Alan Beith paid a visit, where neighbourhood officers updated him. As the weekend approached, there were increasing signs of media hostility; they were restless and impatient at the perceived lack of progress. There was growing resentment, too, from many residents, unhappy at the tactics of some of the larger TV organisations. A Rothbury resident contacted police to outline his concerns. He described most members of the press as 'vultures', hiding in people's gardens and approaching farmers, insinuating they must be frightened and about to arm themselves with their shotguns.

Farmers refused to be drawn on such leading and false assertions.

As Rothbury began a fourth day in lockdown, and the manhunt moved into its seventh day since the shootings at Birtley, the only glimmer of hope in the village was the glorious sunshine; otherwise, it was doom and gloom. Northumbria Police circulated up-to-date CCTV images of Moat, showing a distinctive mohican-style haircut. To maintain some investigative momentum, a Northumbria Police press conference was arranged for the Friday afternoon, with T/Chief Constable Sue Sim and Inspector Sue Peart scheduled to attend.

The people of Rothbury respected and warmed to Mrs Sim, who was highly visible, approachable and supportive of the Rothbury community. She became the public face of Northumbria Police in the hunt for Raoul Moat. At over six-feet tall, her commanding presence towered over her colleagues and her regular media appearances brought instant public recognition. Mrs Sim was known to some sections of the media before the Moat incident. She had previously made no secret of her dislike of trial by media, defending police officers following a G7 international political event in her capacity as public order lead for the Association of Chief Police Officers.

During the Friday press conference, Inspector Peart read the card written by the two schoolchildren that referred to Raoul Moat as a 'nutter'. T/Chief Constable Sim, seated alongside her, smiled as the comments were read. The press conference showed a genuine willingness by police to provide the media with material that reflected the feelings of the wider community. In hindsight, reading the card with the derogatory 'nutter' term was a mistake, at odds with the investigation strategy employed by senior detectives of referring to 'Mr Moat' by surname. Also, the volatility of Moat, in threatening to shoot members of the public for any lies printed in the media, should have guided both T/Chief Constable Sim and Inspector Peart to not read out the children's card. Nonetheless, police press officers were involved, and the senior investigation officer should have been privy to the content of the press briefing. As a result, Northumbria Police apologised for the use of the term 'nutter'.

What was an unfortunate communication mistake served to fuel the worst excesses of the media. Mrs Sim was targeted for her impression of an air stewardess at the public meeting and a minor gaffe at a press briefing, where she stated that she would leave 'every stone unturned' in the hunt for Moat. She was labelled with hostile nicknames comparing her to the Lady Tottingham character from Wallace and Gromit, a barrage of adverse comments referring to her hair and make-up, and now her smirk at the reference to 'nutter'.

Clearly, the chief constable was in a no-win situation with some sections of the media. Mrs Sim, however, showed great determination to stand her ground, rise above the personal abuse and focus on the job in hand, although, of course, she was still only human. A sympathetic pensioner contacted Northumbria Police and offered to pay for the chief constable's haircut from his pension, out of concern for her appearance and her welfare.

Sue Sim joined Merseyside Police as a graduate entrant in 1985, eventually transferred to Northumbria Police in 2004 as Assistant Chief Constable, and there she rose to the position of Deputy Chief Constable. She was promoted to the Temporary Chief Constable vacancy in April 2010. The outcome of the Moat incident would determine the fate of her career, which added further weight to her shoulders. This was compounded by the lack of a breakthrough, which was starting to affect the wider reputation of Northumbria Police.

Mrs Sim had asked an external police force to review Northumbria Police's handling of the ongoing Moat enquiry. I would very much doubt if any other UK police force, faced with the same incident in a similar rural setting, would have achieved a more productive outcome. Indeed, I would hazard a guess that their neighbourhood policing was nowhere near the level of community integration of that already established in Rothbury.

Nonetheless, I was subsequently informed by a senior officer that if Moat was not located within the next 24 hours then the Home Office would relieve T/Chief Constable Sim from overall command of the incident, although she would remain temporary chief. At the end of Friday's press conference, with a lack of progress and an insatiable, destructive media, a tearful Mrs Sim was comforted in private by her colleagues. Her resilience remained strong though; she had earned the trust of the community and had the strength of spirit to overcome these obstacles.

Later that afternoon, Mrs Sim returned to Rothbury to meet up with PC Rob Kilburn, having decided to take time out and accompany the local neighbourhood officer on patrol up the Coquet Valley. As she travelled through the village in her black Range Rover, accompanied by her driver, she noticed almost every inch of grass was occupied by reporters, broadcasting equipment and media satellite vehicles. Mrs Sim was sensitive to the press 'snapping' her on the High Street, when she would have to exchange her staff Range Rover for an armed protected police vehicle. Instead, she decided to rendezvous with PC Kilburn on the hidden gravel track at Riverside, off the main road. At the last minute, the location was changed to the bowls/tennis recreation club car park, just along from the entrance to Riverside.

PC Kilburn and Mrs Sim left the car park and headed up the Coquet Valley, where they patrolled the rural villages of Coquetdale for nearly two hours. The scenic river valley and afternoon sunshine provided some solace and escape from the intensity and heat of Operation Bulwark. They openly talked about their families and how her job would be on the line if they didn't find Moat. Mrs Sim was personable and appreciative of her local officers in their neighbourhood role and the community they served. The operational name Bulwark, in Royal Navy terms, had the motto 'Under thy [God's] wings I will trust'. After seven days, a divine intervention appeared to be the chief constable's only hope, despite the unrelenting efforts of police officers. On returning to Rothbury at around 6:00 pm, Mrs Sim transferred to her staff vehicle in the recreation club car park and returned to force headquarters.

At Rothbury Police Office, PC Lawrie Ward and PC Roxy Bird had started their Friday late shift duty at 5:00 pm. They left the station in a ballistic-protected police vehicle to conduct high-visibility patrols in the village. Armed response officers were also present on the High Street, parked up in their top-of-the range patrol car, appearing relaxed as they enjoyed the summer evening rays.

At around 6:30 pm, the radio dispatcher tasked PCs Ward and Bird to deal with the incident that was on delay from the morning. The caller from Riverside, who reported seeing a suspicious male at 10:30 pm the previous night, had now returned home from work. Both officers returned to the police office shortly before 7:00 pm to view the computerised incident details. PC Ward reviewed the information on the log with the intention of phoning the caller to arrange a visit to her home.

At Riverside, the caller ventured outside her home while waiting for the police to contact her. Unexpectedly, she heard the sound of church bells ringing. The bell ringers of All Saints, Rothbury, no doubt struck a tone of defiance during their regular Friday rehearsal. The lady reflected on the wonderful reassuring feel of the chiming of church bells, which brought an air of normality. Suddenly she was oblivious to the peal of the bells as the same suspicious man from the previous night walked past her, heading along the path in the direction of Rothbury. He was tall and well-built in stature but was wearing different clothing. For no apparent reason the man immediately changed direction and darted behind a tree, as if to avoid being seen. The woman hastily retreated inside her house to phone the police. As she was about to dial the emergency number, her phone started ringing; it was PC Lawrie Ward. 'He's there now!' she instinctively blurted out.

PC Ward, whether through experience, intuition or pure instinct, knew the suspicious male was Moat. The officer told the caller to stay in the house: 'Police will be there straight away.' PC Ward hung up and darted from the police office. PC Bird was otherwise engaged so he took a Berwick probationer officer, who happened to be loitering in the front office, with him. As a Rothbury neighbourhood officer, Lawrie knew the exact location on Riverside. Having just been on patrol in the village, he also knew an armed response vehicle from West Yorkshire Police was parked at the bottom of the High Street, which was en route to Riverside. PC Ward attempted to inform the control room, but due to radio traffic instead opted to press his emergency button, which silenced the airwaves and gave him a ten-second period to transmit the reported sighting.

The officer was concerned the incident would be delayed by control room supervision in order to re-contact the caller, conduct an untimely risk assessment, or direct armed response officers, with limited local knowledge of the exact location, to the scene. Single-minded in his determination, PC Ward took the decision and drove the armoured police vehicle at speed down Rothbury High Street. On passing the West Yorkshire armed response vehicle, PC Ward and his colleague signalled for the armed officers to follow. PC Ward turned right into Riverside, closely followed by his armed colleagues.

Directly in front was a narrow strip of grass with the tree-lined riverbank behind. The officers turned right, to head along the gravel path, with the grassed area and river to their left. Almost instantly, PC Ward noticed the man as described, wearing dark grey clothing and a baseball cap. He was walking across the grass 15 metres away, near a cluster of riverbank trees and bushes. Almost instantly, the suspect put his hand inside a plastic bag he was carrying and took out what was clearly a sawn-off shotgun. He pointed the gun to the side of his head, fell to his knees and lay motionless on the ground with the end of the gun trained on his head and his finger firmly on the trigger.

Armed response officers, on seeing the suspect, got out their car and took up armed positions to contain the man. The officers used the ballistic-protected Northern Irish police carrier as cover, while PC Ward and his colleague remained secure inside. The suspect was threatening suicide if any officer approached.

He remained unmoving and silent on the grass in front of a tree, with the river directly behind, the shotgun pointed to the side of his head. Police weapons were trained on his every move; the situation was at a stand-off. The manhunt for the fugitive Raoul Moat was over.

The village tranquillity was abruptly shattered by the spontaneous sounding of police sirens as more armed officers and local police units travelled to the scene. On the High Street, the nervous reaction of residents and the scrambling of the media created a panic situation. A police dog vehicle collided with another car during the mayhem – the vexed police Alsatian must have wondered what the hell was going on.

Uniform police arrived on foot to close the roads leading to Riverside, and officers erected cordons to create a sterile area to protect the scene. Residents gathered on the main street, joined by dozens of reporters. Impromptu live broadcasts took place, much to the frustration of police who were trying to close the road for the safety of the public. Lines of police officers ushered the media and residents along the street towards the Jubilee Hall and the junction with Bridge Street. Several bloodthirsty reporters had other ideas and completely ignored police directions; reporters ran across the bridge and headed towards the old mart buildings and stepping stones to get an improved gantry position on the opposite side of the river.

PC Ward urgently requested via his police radio that the exit route from Riverside, over the stepping stones, was blocked off by firearms officers. On hearing a radio message that police had firearms on Moat, PC Rob Kilburn and PC Roxy Bird, with their detailed knowledge of the area, ran down the High Street to help orchestrate cordons. PC Bird described elements of the media as 'behaving like locusts' and of ignoring her repeated directions, causing the officer at one point to break down in tears. Reporters even secreted themselves in bushes, shouting across the river, 'Look this way, Raoul'. The lack of press standards and decency knew no bounds.

With the arrival of additional police officers, the main roads and bridge were closed and the immediate area sealed off. Armed police were in position and the gunman was surrounded on all sides. Moat remained steadfast, lying on his front on the grass with the shotgun fixed to the side of his head, showing a clear intention to blast himself if any officer came too close.

Rothbury Neighbourhood Officer PC Ward and his colleague were withdrawn from the scene under the protection of armed officers. Two other local officers who were taking statements at a nearby house also removed themselves from address, out of harm's way. The situation was at a pause, bringing an element of calm and composure to the scene, pending the arrival of specialist police negotiators.

The force and community could at last breathe a sigh of relief, thanks in no small part to the intuitive response and bravery of PC Lawrie Ward and his student officer colleague, both of whom were instrumental in bringing an end to the terror. Word of Moat's capture reached an extremely relieved T/Chief Constable Sim as she travelled to Northumbria Police Headquarters, having just left Rothbury less than an hour before Moat's discovery. Divine intervention indeed.

PC Ward and his colleague were unharmed, and both officers returned to Rothbury Police Station, no doubt full of excited emotion and personal satisfaction at the part they played in the capture of Raoul Thomas Moat. While there were no formal post-incident management procedures conducted with the officers, the consummate professional Inspector Peart carried out post-incident 'defusing' with each, in support of their welfare. Both officers were allowed to terminate duty just after 8:00 pm – not a bad shift at all!

A relieved PC Lawrie Ward returned home to his family and the sounds of his son: 'Dad! Dad! Have you got him yet, Dad? Have you got him?'

This time, Lawrie answered with immense pride, 'Yes, son, I got him.'

5
STAND-OFF

Police secured the scene, closed nearby roads and set up cordons to establish a sterile area. Armed officers encircled the grassy knoll where Moat lay, deathly still with his gun to his head. Rothbury Bridge and the adjacent Bridge Street were closed, and across the river police officers evicted several irresponsible members of the press who were hiding in bushes, trying to attract Moat's attention for that exclusive photograph or comment. Moat remained unperturbed, lying on his front on the grass. He was surrounded by armed police officers with semi-automatic guns and telescopic rifles: an insurmountable array of weaponry and deadly force.

With the centre of the village and the bridge sealed off, locals drinking at the Railway Hotel on Bridge Street were stranded inside, unable to leave, although I'm sure there were worse places to be marooned, as the beer continued to flow from the taps. A wedding reception at the Coquetvale Hotel, situated on the opposite side of the river, was also interrupted, as the caterers were unable to cross the bridge to deliver food. As residents gathered on the High Street, the pleasant summer's evening had an air of apprehension and nervous tension while people waited for news of any further developments. Television and radio programming across all national and local networks gave way to live broadcasts from Rothbury, with rolling news coverage and instant 'expert analysis'. The final scenes would be played out in front of a worldwide audience, and viewers watched in anticipation and suspense to see how the Moat story would end.

Northumbria Police were fortunate that enough firearms resources were available for deployment, as numerous armed officers had been given time off after working continuous 18-hour shifts. Specialist sniper officers were in position, as well as police equipped with less lethal weapons, including Taser. The intention was to take Moat alive; however, if firearms officers were required to stop an armed Moat leaving the scene, or if he presented a danger to the public or police officers, there was to be no hesitation in officers using lawful force to stop the threat. The lesser option of shooting Moat in the limbs was not under consideration. That decision rested with firearms officers at the scene alone and was not predetermined by Silver Command.

One concern was the ability of the standard sidearm Taser gun to successfully strike Moat from a police negotiating distance, as it would be at the limits of its capabilities. There was a need for a more effective, less lethal, option to prevent Moat from shooting himself. Police have a legal duty to protect human life, including Raoul Moat's life, despite his intention to kill himself.

A suggestion was made to senior officers to use the XREP (Extended Range Electronic Projectile) Taser, whose reach of 100 feet was four times that of a standard police Taser. Instead of the two wired metal barbs fired from the police-issue Taser into the target, the XREP uses shotgun-type cartridges that fire barbs into the subject and discharge high-voltage electricity to the body, causing incapacitation. Northumbria Police were apparently already in possession of a XREP Taser, having acquired the weapon following a demonstration by an American commercial company.

Following legal consideration, chief officers authorised the use of the unproven X-12 XREP Taser as a means of last resort to save the life of Raoul Moat. Although the weapon was not approved for operational use by the Home Office, it provided the only practical means of intervening if Moat was about to pull the trigger on himself.

Northumbria Police urgently sought the requisition of XREP Tasers from Pro-Tect Systems, a UK supplier based in Northampton, in the East Midlands. The weapon's discharge was similar to a shotgun, but firearms officers had never seen, held, fired or had any formal training on the X-12 Taser. Following delivery of the new weapons, and while Moat remained prone on the grass with the gun to his head, selected officers were given five minutes ad hoc use of the weapon at a makeshift training range that was set up at the RVP on the industrial estate. Senior officers searched the internet to find out more information on the weapon but were hampered by poor internet connectivity in Rothbury. As experienced police negotiators liaised with Moat at the scene, seeking to establish a rapport, the force hoped that the XREP Taser would not be needed.

The role of the police negotiators was to resolve the situation peacefully. The process would involve dialogue with Moat – to gather information or buy time to review decisions and determine further negotiating tactics to be used. Negotiating officers were trained at different levels of expertise depending on the type of situation, with regional and national coordination networks in place to support best practice. Northumbria Police negotiators had spent 14 hours working as a pair, rehearsing for

such a stand-off situation. They agreed that the principal negotiator (Number 1) would communicate and negotiate with the
subject. The second negotiator (Number 2) would observe, listen and feed information through an earpiece to the principal.

The grassed scene, partly enclosed by trees and foliage, served
as an amphitheatre in which negotiators could calmly and
quietly converse with Moat without undue distraction. The
presence of armed officers positioned nearby, using the cover
of vehicles, ballistic shields and trees for protection, resolutely
emphasised the 'end game' while allowing the space and time to
seek a peaceful resolution.

Moat remained motionless, lying on the ground with his
sawn-off shotgun fixed to the side of his head as police negotiators attempted to build a rapport. He spoke calmly and ration-
ally, repeating several times that he didn't want to go back to
prison. Moat talked about himself and his ex-partner Samantha
Stobbart, but not his other victims Chris Brown or PC David
Rathband, as if they were inconsequential to him. Negotiators
sought to reassure him, while acknowledging he would do some
time: 'What will your family, your grandmother, think? What
do they want?' Moat reiterated that this would end tonight,
leading police to believe that a possible 'suicide by cop' situation
could be the outcome – Moat could threaten police with his
shotgun, resulting in a lethal return of fire.

Police negotiations were conducted in a structured way
within a planned negotiating strategy, and the officers felt that a
good rapport had been established. Any negotiating situation is
imprecise in nature and can spontaneously change course without notice, presenting an immediate risk to both police and the
subject. The introduction of a third party, such as a relative or

friend, brings a further element of potential risk and is generally avoided unless the negotiators are of the belief that such an exceptional tactic would safely resolve a situation. A close friend of Moat was permitted access through the cordon in the hope his presence would persuade Moat to give himself up. He had known Moat since childhood and had spent many happy times with him, fishing in local rivers, and they had a shared interest in body building. The friend had last spoken with Moat earlier in the week while he was on the run; however, the police negotiators refused to let him speak directly with the gunman.

Former England and Newcastle United footballer Paul Gascoigne, also known as Gazza, travelled by taxi from Newcastle, arriving at Rothbury around 10:00 pm, in the belief he could talk Moat into handing himself over to police. Gazza was a recovering alcoholic and appeared inebriated, high on drink and cocaine. He had brought Moat a dressing gown, a jacket, chicken, a fishing rod and a can of lager.

On arrival at a police checkpoint just outside Rothbury, Gazza tried to persuade officers that he was a personal friend of Moat, having met him on the doors at nightclubs in Newcastle. Gazza was familiar with the river at Rothbury and intended to take Moat fishing: 'I guarantee Moaty, he won't shoot me, I am good friends with him,' he slurred. Police politely smiled and turned him away. He headed back to Newcastle, but not before making a live cameo interview on a local radio station. Gazza woke up the following morning, without any recollection of events, and later admitted he had never met Raoul Moat. For all his demons linked to alcohol and drug dependency he was well-meaning, and drew a sympathetic response from the British public. I just hope Gazza doesn't bring a Ray Mears-inspired book out, claiming to have been within a whisker of persuading Moat to hand himself over to police!

As police negotiations continued, the rapport with Moat was described as amicable, respectful and conciliatory in tone. Moat told police where he had hidden a gun in the woods, as he did not want a child to find it. 'Do you mind if I sit up?' Moat asked as he took sandwiches.

Northumbria Police negotiators spent over two hours talking to Moat and they were convinced he would put the gun down and hand himself over to them. For understandable, but rather bewildering, reasons, negotiator Number 2 – who was accredited to regional standard and had detailed knowledge of Moat, having established a rapport up to that point – was unexpectedly replaced by a new Number 2 from another police force, who was accredited to the higher national standard. The principal negotiator (Number 1) was concerned that he wouldn't get anything like the same level of background knowledge or detail to support the ongoing negotiations with Moat. As darkness fell and midnight approached, heavy rainfall put a dampener on negotiations and the riverside setting. The scene was now illuminated by portable lighting, with the distant humming of a generator disturbing the serenity of night. Moat's mental state and inner thoughts were unclear. He remained passive, perhaps reflecting – how did it come to this?

Psychologists identify internalising and externalising behaviours, both of which were evident in Moat's thought processes. Externalising was exhibited at the start of his rampage when he blamed everyone other than himself for his behaviour: Northumbria Police and social services for destroying his life and making him serve time in prison; and Samantha Stobbart for ending their relationship, leading, as Moat would reason, to him shooting Stobbart Chris Brown and PC David Rathband:

Yeah, well, I'm gonna destroy a few lives like you destroyed mine. This is what happens when you push, push and push …

At some point, Moat's externalising of his behaviour gave way to the internalising of his own thoughts. Reality kicked in and he looked inwards to himself, his own actions, his responsibility, and the severity of the consequences he must now face. There was no hiding – the time was nigh.

SATURDAY, 10 JULY

As midnight passed, the darkened atmosphere and rain-drenched scene reflected the gloom overhanging the police negotiation. It was almost at an impasse and there was a sense of it having run its course. Moat was subdued and anxious, reiterating that he did not want to go to jail. 'It is going to end in this field tonight,' he said, never letting go of the gun, the barrel touching the side of his head and his finger glued to the trigger. Haunting words, permanently etched in the minds of the armed officers who remained steadfast in their containment, their weapons trained on every move Moat made.

Six hours into the stand-off, at around 1:15 am, in the early hours of a dismal wet Saturday morning, police officers were gravely concerned at his mental state. Moat was seen to shuffle his feet as if to stand up, and he repositioned the gun upwards from under his chin and towards his temple. Police Taser officers, believing Moat was about to kill himself, discharged the X-12 Taser, aiming at his chest. Moat let out a noise as if he had been struck. He rocked back, lifted his shotgun up at an angle and blasted a gunshot to the side of his head. Moat fell backwards into the long grass, fatally wounded with serious head injuries, the gun by his side.

Surrounding armed police officers immediately charged towards Moat, shouting repeat warnings as they secured possession of his gun to protect themselves. Moat appeared lifeless on the ground. No police firearms other than the Taser were discharged, and ambulance paramedics, on standby outside the inner cordon, were called up to the scene. Police officers and paramedics pulled his body clear of the long grass and desperately tried to save his life.

A differing version of the events rumoured to have taken place later came to light. During the stand-off, Moat claimed that the police spotlights that were illuminating the night-time scene were too bright and requested they be dimmed, but the police officer controlling the lights inadvertently switched them all off. The scene fell into complete darkness for a split second. The officer instinctively turned the lights back on, lighting up the scene in a flash, which caused Moat to react and lift the gun to his head. Police discharged their Taser weapons in the belief that Moat was about to kill himself, leading to Moat firing the shotgun and inflicting fatal injuries.

I can't state whether this alternative version is factual or just a rumour without any substance or truth. I was not present at the scene and can't give testimony to the chronological events leading to Moat's death. Suffice to say, the circumstances leading to the discharge of Taser weapons were the subject of an extensive IPCC investigation, and the cause of Moat's death was determined following a coroner's inquest. The actions of the force and officers at the scene were deemed lawful, necessary and proportionate, with the clear intention to preserve life.

Moat, having suffered serious head injuries, was rushed to Newcastle General Hospital by ambulance under police escort. His condition was critical and he was pronounced dead shortly after arrival, at 2:20 am. At Northumbria Police Headquarters, a rather elated T/Chief Constable Sim embraced and kissed officers returning from the scene as if they were soldiers returning from the front line. Professionally, the force maintained that their preference was to capture Moat alive and put him on trial, but his self-inflicted death was 'reputationally manageable' as an alternative outcome. Silver Commander Superintendent Jo Farrell was also relieved as the seven-day manhunt ended abruptly. The IPCC launched an investigation following mandatory referral from Northumbria Police.

The scene was preserved, pending the arrival of an IPCC investigation team, and post-incident firearms procedures were implemented to secure evidence and support officer welfare. Some identification numbers provided by armed personnel at the scene, requested for the crime scene logs, were more akin to the military than police. The firearms officers were stood down after a lengthy and emotionally draining stand-off. High levels of responsibility and personal accountability had been placed on their shoulders – the decision to use lethal force, or Tasers, was theirs alone. A firearms officer who was present during the final stages said that the conversation with Moat was all about himself and what would happen to him: 'Never in a million miles did I think he would shoot himself,' he said.

The area of Riverside remained sealed off, with cordons in place and a forensic tent erected to protect the scene. Local officer PC Rob Kilburn was finally able to terminate duty nearly 24 hours after he started, almost as an afterthought. As a Rothbury officer, Rob felt sidelined as he stood for hours on a police cordon. His local knowledge could have been put to better use in preparing the daytime community police response. In the village, the world's media were milling around, broadcasting live early-morning news feeds to satisfy an insatiable public appetite. Newspaper headlines read 'CORNERED' and 'GOT HIM'.[3]

Interestingly, an American visitor to London expressed his surprise at Moat's death being headline news. 'In the USA, this would not hit the papers. There would be no extended negotiation – Moat would be shot,' he said. The handling by UK police officers reflected a marked difference in the freedoms and human rights between the two countries and, of course, the gun culture. No matter how serious his criminality, Moat's right to life was protected in law as enshrined in the European Convention on Human Rights. The professionalism, restraint and compassion exercised by Northumbria Police bear testimony to the proudest traditions of the British police service in going the second mile to try to safeguard the life of Moat.

Raoul Thomas Moat had a choice not afforded to Christopher Brown, Samantha Stobbart or PC David Rathband. Despite assertions he had a mental illness, Moat had the mental capacity to make judgements. He took a decision to end his own life, as opposed to handing himself over to police to face justice. Family and friends of Moat will understandably mourn his loss, but

---

3   Daily Mail, July2010, 'Cornered' Available online [Accessed Nov 2019]; The Sun, July2010, 'Got Him' Available online [Accessed Nov 2019]

they should not portray Moat as the victim in circumstances he created. Moat was responsible for his actions and his self-inflicted death, which ended seven days of fear and terror across Tyneside and Northumberland.

As the sun rose over Rothbury, the community awoke to a new dawn and a chance to renew and start afresh; somehow, normality would never be the same again.

6
NORMALITY

As the early-morning sun peered down on the village, a renewed confidence filled the air as shopkeepers opened up in anticipation of the resumption of normal Saturday trading. Residents began to appear on the High Street, forming clusters outside the newsagents and smiling as pleasantries were exchanged. No doubt they also reflected on the death of Moat, which brought an end to a week of turmoil, with a new sense of freedom and optimism. 'We can now get our lives back,' as one resident mildly put it. The Riverside area was sealed off and secured by officers waiting for the arrival of staff from the IPCC. The media were prevalent in the village throughout the morning, broadcasting final news reports from their pop-up gazebos, with an eye on clearing up and returning home; some residents were glad to wave them off with a sense of 'good riddance' – they were pleased to see the back of them.

Just after 7:00 am, I set out from home in possession of a pushchair and my two-year-old daughter, Elsi, heading, not to Rothbury, but south to the magnificent cathedral city of Durham to attend the annual Durham Miners' Gala. The parade of the many colliery brass bands and banners through the streets of Durham represents the embodiment of community strength and togetherness in overcoming adversity, where people and communities matter. Similarities can be drawn with the people of Rothbury. What became so apparent was the impact of the Moat incident on the people and communities across the wider North East of England. Durham Constabulary police officers, milling around at 8:00 am awaiting the arrival of the thousands of gala visitors, expressed relief that the trauma of Moat was over, even though they were not directly involved. It may have just been an emotional reaction, but the air smelt fresher, visitors laughed louder, and the brass bands sounded brighter with greater musical clarity. The ripples of normality would spread from Rothbury, touching people from all communities across the UK.

At Rothbury, there was a sense of relief, not just in the community, but among senior officers of Northumbria Police, and especially T/Chief Constable Sue Sim. The outcome, in effect, saved her job and significantly improved her prospects of being appointed permanently to the vacant chief constable position. Inspector Sue Peart probably woke up a little chirpier too, having suffered the critical media response to her 'nutter' comment made at the press conference the previous day. Chief Superintendent Mark Dennett and PC Trevor Weldon joined the inspector at the follow-up Critical IAG meeting, held at 11:00 am that Saturday morning. Local community partners were in attendance, albeit fewer in number with the incident having concluded. The only issue discussed was the return to normality. The attendees were highly appreciative of Northumbria Police taking the time to consult with them and keep them informed. Inspector Peart expressed her sincere gratitude for their support.

Investigation officers from the IPCC began arriving at the scene and took up residence at Rothbury Police Office. The

IPCC focus was on two distinct areas of examination: the acquisition, use, authorisation and deployment of the XREP Tasers; and the prison release warning notification concerning Moat and subsequent actions taken by Northumbria Police. The two-mile radial exclusion and air exclusion zone remained in force, but police officers temporarily deployed to Rothbury now returned to their previously assigned stations. Specialist police search units, assisted by Northumberland National Park Mountain Rescue Team, continued to search for a discarded shotgun in the extensive grounds of Cragside Estate, and detectives followed up intelligence on the whereabouts of Moat while on the run.

Neighbourhood officers, supported by operational support resources (dogs, traffic and the mounted section), focused on community reassurance, with Operation Ayden replacing Operation Bulwark. Key media messages were disseminated, and high-visibility patrols conducted. Mounted police horses trotted up and down the High Street, their statuesque presence also gracing the scenic riverbank. Community impact assessments were updated and reviewed by senior officers to determine the mood of the community and identify any tensions or local concerns. As the vibrancy of rural life emerged over the weekend, rural residents, tourists and the increased vehicle congestion brought an appearance of a village back on its feet. The peal of the church bells on Sunday morning, sounding across the rooftops and beckoning the community to come together in spirit and harmony, epitomised the feeling.

PC Trevor Weldon attended the Sunday morning service at All Saints Church, Rothbury, immaculately dressed in his police tunic, in keeping with the best traditions of the force. Presiding at the service of thanksgiving was the Archdeacon of Lindisfarne. The Holy Island of Lindisfarne in Northumberland is of significant importance in bringing the Gospel of Christianity to England. The presence, strength and voice of the church in times of need and insecurity is a sanctuary of comfort, reassurance and hope. With village life slowly returning to normal, and the media having left, Northumbria Police released the following community statement:

Monday 12 July 2010

The protection of the public has always been our number one priority throughout this enquiry. We did everything we could to ensure the situation was brought to a safe conclusion. We would like to thank the residents of Rothbury for their overwhelming support during what has been a very difficult time. Your patience and understanding has been invaluable.

We are also grateful to the members of the public who have provided us with information to assist in our investigation. Although we are thankful that the incident has been brought to a close, we are mindful of the impact it has had on many lives. An innocent member of the public has been killed; another innocent member of the public has been seriously injured and one of our colleagues has also been seriously injured. Our thoughts are with the family and friends of those affected.

PC Rathband's condition is stable and comfortable. Samantha Stobbart is poorly. They have both been kept fully informed of developments. As police had contact with Moat prior to his death, the incident has been referred to the IPCC, as is required in such circumstances.

It is now time for a return to normality in Rothbury and all our communities affected by events in the last seven days.

Managing normality from a neighbourhood police perspective resembled the aftermath of floods and other major incidents, with the focus on vulnerability and public reassurance. The Raoul Moat incident severely affected the Rothbury community and beyond. Clearly, some individuals were feeling traumatised, insecure and frightened. The healing process would take time and our first priority was to identify those residents, victims and witnesses in need of support, whether through a welfare visit by an officer, or referral to specialist victim support services. In mind was the victim of the burglary dwelling at Walby Hill, where a footprint was found inside the house (subsequently identified as an exact match to the footwear worn by Raoul Moat); owners of buildings believed to have been entered by the gunman; a female resident who had a previous friendship with Moat; and residents in the immediate vicinity of Riverside, where the grassy knoll death scene was the centre of world attention.

In consultation with Rothbury doctors surgery, local authority partners and members of the community, a list of potentially vulnerable residents was created with a view to making contact to check on their wellbeing. Surprisingly, a phone call was received from the British Red Cross, offering their services to visit people affected by Moat. The organisation had recently supported and comforted the victims of the Derrick Bird shooting, where 12 members of the public were killed in the neighbouring county of Cumbria, a few weeks before. The offer was gratefully accepted and home visits were conducted by neighbourhood officers, British Red Cross volunteers or victim support staff, with onward referral to specialist health services where a need was identified. The contribution from the British Red Cross was outstanding, and police and the community were thankful.

With the last remnants of media intrusion having now left the village, the event continued to make headlines in national newspapers and across all television networks. Relatives of Moat featured prominently, including his older brother, tax officer Angus Moat:

> 'It was like a public execution, I'm probably the only person who has ever witnessed their brother die live on national television. I wouldn't wish that on anyone, especially when you can't do anything about it.'[4]

While his emotive response was understandable, it would appear Angus Moat had a sudden re-evaluation of his relationship with his brother following his death, claiming that he should have been given the opportunity to talk his sibling into surrendering to police. This was rather surprising as Angus had been estranged from Raoul Moat for seven years. Police had believed that a confrontation between the brothers may have inflamed the situation.

Family members, although no doubt well meaning, might have gained a greater understanding of the outcome by reflecting on the impact of their own family relationship breakdown on the behaviour of Moat.

It was far from a public execution. Police made painstaking steps to save Moat's life. The only executions in this tragic event involved Moat: the cowardly shooting dead of Chris Brown; attempting to kill Samantha Stobbart; and the cold-blooded attempted murder of PC David Rathband.

---

4   'Brother angry over Raoul Moat death.' ITN News (July 2010). Available from www.youtube.com/watch?v=-KHy66PFeBk [Accessed Nov 2019]

Unlike his victims, Raoul Moat was able to determine his own fate.

Community anger was still simmering, directed towards some elements of press reporting and social media content. In contrast, there was immense praise and gratitude afforded to Northumbria Police, as commented by Farm Watch members:

'I think the police acted professionally under difficult circumstances. I agree it is a shame he was not taken alive but nobody can stop someone determined to end their life.'

'I express my sympathy to PC Rathband, he is an excellent man, I hope his sight recovers.'

'Talk of a legend [Moat] is offensive and cannot be understood. He was a murderer and should be treated as such.'

'I believe the outcome was inevitable. It is a shame that so much money will be spent on a review of how police acted. All so easy after the event, so police have my support for what it is worth.'

'For the record, I truly appreciate the police keeping the people of Rothbury safe. Not one person has said anything but praise – pass on my thanks.'

Northumberland County Councillor Steven Bridgett was inundated with letters and compliments from members of the public expressing their appreciation of Northumbria Police, which he conveyed to Chief Superintendent Mark Dennett. Relations between police and the people of Rothbury had been strengthened through adversity, with an unwavering bond of trust persevering throughout. A cash reward of £10,000, offered by Northumbria Police for information leading to the capture of Moat, was paid out in a low-key visit to the resident concerned.

As a clear sign of intent for the village to move on, preparations began for the annual Rothbury Traditional Music Festival, scheduled to take place on the weekend after hostilities ended. Visiting Northumbrian folk musicians, ceilidh bands, local craft events, and a parade by the Rothbury Highland Pipe Band would collectively serve to bring the community together in song, harmony and wellbeing. Somehow, music has the means to melt the frozen ice within us all. The timing of the weekend festival and influx of visitors supported a return to normality; albeit in an atmosphere of contrasting celebration and cautious anticipation, with Rothbury having lost a little of its idyllic charm.

With businesses, shops and schools coming back to life, neighbourhood police officers maintained a highly visible presence. Although the local authority had fully cleansed the human-scarred landscape, the site was now a mecca for visitors and a new tourist attraction had emerged. Like Dallas in the USA, where President John F Kennedy was assassinated, Rothbury too had an infamous 'grassy knoll'. Visitors gathered at the site, taking pictures and laying floral tributes at a shrine in memory of Raoul Moat, who had become a cult figure to some, to the exasperation of local residents and the wider public. Tributes left at the scene read:

'RAOUL MOAT – TRUE LEGEND'

'RIP. MR MOAT Totally understand your feelings. God Bless X'

'RAOUL – Gone but not forgotten, a true Gent They Never Took You RIP.'

The laying of flowers became a particular area of grievance

and potential conflict. Many residents felt that visitors leaving tributes in memory of a murderer who shot and seriously injured a police officer was distasteful, intimidating and disrespectful to the community. An irate county councillor, Steven Bridgett, attached two notices on council letterheads to trees at the scene to deter such activity. In doing so, Councillor Bridgett received a stern rebuke from Northumberland County Council, who stated it was not acceptable to post a document on official county council letter-headed paper without proper authority. They stated the action could have provoked an already tense situation. A youthful, rather dismissive, Councillor Bridgett claimed he was simply asking that anyone coming to the site show some respect for the residents that live in his community.

Bizarrely, a mother of eight children travelled to the scene from her home in Surrey, wearing a Chelsea football top and accompanied by her three sons, having never met the killer. She said:

> I absolutely loved him. I just think he is a hero and just wanted to pay my respects. He kept them coppers on the run for all of that time. Fair enough people died but they must have deserved it.[5]

An incomprehensible, feckless and irresponsible statement. The mind boggles.

Facebook tribute pages were set up in memory of Moat, with comments of similar intellect. The issue became the subject of political debate in the House of Commons at Westminster, with condemnation from Prime Minister David Cameron. Facebook

---

5 'Raoul's ghouls.' *The Mail* online (August 2010). Available from www.dailymail.co.uk/news/article-1299709/Raoul-Moat-fans-met-fugitive-killer-flock-funeral-hero.html [Accessed Nov 2019]

refused to take down the web pages, providing a statement in response:

> Facebook is a place where people can express their views and discuss things in an open way as they can and do in many other places, and as such we sometimes find people discussing topics others may find distasteful; however, that is not a reason in itself to stop a debate from happening.

Facebook may serve as a catalyst for free speech, but it is also a platform for perpetrators of unlawful abuse and malicious communications, where they appear to operate with impunity.

Tributes left at the scene in commemoration of Moat were removed during the night by unknown local people; however, some flowers were respectfully repositioned to a secluded corner in the local church cemetery. Police considered the installation of covert cameras to oversee the scene and monitor visitors and any potential criminal behaviour. The grassed area was privately owned land, of which Northumberland County Council had assumed oversight. The council determined that all dead flowers would be removed until, gradually, the placing of floral tributes ceased. The landscape would be allowed to reconfigure, with the grass left to grow, and the trees and shrubs pruned back to change the look of the site. Local Neighbourhood Environmental Action Teams were directed to 'blitz' and fully cleanse the village. The official focus was on the forthcoming weekend of music festivities to support the folk musicians, ceilidhs and events taking place in and around Rothbury.

While Rothbury welcomed music festival visitors, the sudden influx of outsiders sympathetic to Moat was noticeable. Several showed a complete lack of respect or sensitivity towards local residents, and rumours on social networking sites raised concerns that a busload of Moat's friends were planning to visit Rothbury over the festival weekend, 'looking for justice'. A telephone call was made to a pub in the village: 'Have you got lots of beer? Cos thousands of us are coming for a Raoul Moat Memorial Day, dressed as chickens and as Gazza, carrying fishing rods.' An elderly resident reported her unease with a male 'visitor' when standing outside the carpet shop on the High Street. She overheard him commenting on the glass windows, implying that damage would be caused to the shop. Three other men, who were clearly not locals, approached a resident and said, 'Do you live here? Do you think it is fucking funny?'

Northumbria Police motor patrols policed the main arterial roads to and from Rothbury. Automatic number plate recognition technology (ANPR) was used to scan vehicles heading towards the area, for intelligence purposes and to identify criminality. Several occupants of a car had travelled over 50 miles from Murton, County Durham, to visit Rothbury to commemorate Moat. Local officers on patrol in the village challenged the individuals, who were directed to leave. As they drove away from Rothbury, an ANPR motor patrols camera was activated, which flagged that they didn't have insurance. The vehicle was stopped and seized by police and the occupants were left by the roadside, to continue their journey home on foot.

Numerous reports were also received of visitors sympathetic to Moat attending Rothbury Riverside at all times, especially during the night. The grassy knoll and surrounding riverbank were 'lit up like a Christmas tree'. Car headlights and the repeated flashing of cameras captured visitors posing, drinking and laughing. A number of elderly residents living nearby found the behaviour intimidating.

Northumbria Police introduced a memorandum of understanding in seeking to define the boundaries of acceptable behaviour. The force recognised that policing was by the consent of the local community, with the need to reassure them in difficult circumstances, balanced with a freedom of expression, where there may be opposing viewpoints to those of the local community.

Operation Ayden was the force's response to managing community tensions during the transition to normality. The highly visible presence of local officers on foot, and the comforting sound of an officer on a police horse, served to reassure the community and deter the inconsiderate, ignorant behaviour of a few. Any visitor who presented with undesirable motives was challenged, and officers engaged with those attending the scene in support of Moat, to ensure a mutual understanding of acceptable behaviour. Any provocative T-shirts, inappropriate language or conduct were disrupted to prevent friction.

Police contingencies were in place; public-order-equipped officers were in position at the nearby Rothbury Community Hospital in anticipation of a call to bear down on any escalating situation in the village. Intelligence-led patrols, welfare visits to residents, police visibility at key points, licensing checks, assertive media messages and continuous reviews of community impact assessments all served to keep disruption to a minimum.

The Rothbury Traditional Music Festival took place in glorious weather. Visitor numbers were high and the event exceeded all expectations. Performers, musicians and tourists flocked to the weekend festivities at various venues, and ad hoc open-air performances, ceilidh events and music groups, who performed on the outdoor stage, all delighted the record numbers of people attending. The sunny weather and celebratory atmosphere led to the event being one of the most successful and enjoyable festivals in its history, with no adverse incidents of note. Normality was returning, slowly but surely.

As policing adjusted to 'business as usual', officer welfare remained a priority consideration. Post-incident support was provided by Northumbria Police Occupation Health Unit, and arrangements were made for local officers to be given the opportunity to talk with senior occupational health counsellors in a confidential setting. This provided an outlet for shared experiences and helped identify any further support needed. The consultations were held away from the police station environment, which enabled officers to open up about personal feelings, anxieties and emotions on what had been a momentous roller-coaster journey. Across the force, traumatised victims, witnesses and members of the public remained a focus for police support, especially those who had a direct involvement with Moat, and access to specialist victim support services was offered.

T/Chief Constable Sue Sim intended to hold a wide-ranging force debrief to identify learning areas for the organisation. The scope of any debrief was curtailed due to ongoing IPCC enquiries and criminal proceedings, but Rothbury Neighbourhood Officers held a debrief at the nearby Cragside House and a report was submitted to Northumbria Police Headquarters, outlining key areas of concern from a local policing perspective. These included:

> Area Command officers (unarmed) were directed to attend incidents and search locations within proximity to Moat.
>
> Negligible buy-in of local police knowledge was sought or given prominence.

Incidents of sightings of Moat were delayed, with follow-up enquiries by unarmed uniformed officers (one incident resulted in locating Moat).

Silo leadership structures, with no forward control point in Rothbury, which would have allowed supervision on the ground to communicate, share information and local knowledge.

The restrictive ability of the force to process a significant volume of incident information and intelligence.

Senior investigation officers informed the media that there was now a threat to the public from Moat, which had not clearly been communicated to officers tasked to reassure the public.

Northumberland National Park Authority, who provided local knowledge and mountain rescue search team volunteers, requested a debrief to highlight learning areas, which included communication issues and a lack of feedback. Despite repeated requests and an agreement by senior officers for such a debrief to be held, the meeting never materialised.

Assistant Chief Constable Steve Ashman, as Gold Commander during the Moat incident, toured the force area to conduct a series of talks with police officers involved. His aim was to value their contributions and provide a broader operational overview and the rationale for decisions made. Rothbury and Alnwick neighbourhood officers attended the meeting, held at Alnwick Police Station. Mr Ashman's talk included the reason for sanctioning XREP Tasers (as a last resort to save life) and the nightmare situation in having to protect unarmed officers, the community and schools from an armed Moat intending to kill. The unrestrained behaviour of sections of the national media was also discussed, and how Moat and his accomplices had been parked outside McDonald's at Ashington, watching unarmed female officers returning to the nearby police station. Whatever the concerns of officers during the incident, in particular officer safety, colleagues were appreciative of the time taken by Mr Ashman in explaining and providing a wider understanding of the decisions taken. This served to dissipate any lingering doubts or resentments.

Chief Superintendent Dennett requested a detailed overview of all aspects of the work undertaken by the neighbourhood police team. The commanding officer had spoken with senior Whitehall officials at the Home Office in London and the government had requested the information, to be held as an example of best practice in community policing, for which some national recognition was being proposed. 'Let's get it down on paper,' he said.

In the weeks that followed, Rothbury returned to a post-Moat normality. All media had deserted the village and local policing had gravitated back to neighbourhood officers. Businesses and tourists enjoyed the final trading and leisure opportunities of an eventful summer; however, the mental scars affecting people in the community would take longer to heal, as Rothbury was now in a different place emotionally, having lost its quaint village character.

Not one to miss out on a positive media opportunity, the government minister for crime prevention, James Brokenshire MP, visited Northumbria Police to personally thank officers for their work on the Moat incident. A gathering of officers, police staff and volunteers was hastily arranged at Cragside House, Rothbury. It was interesting looking around the packed room, reflecting on the part played by colleagues, including some of the senior police officers in attendance who had worked at arm's length from the front line. As with the government minister, they were likely first-time visitors to Rothbury, maybe looking at promotion or with career networking and portfolio building on their minds.

From a community perspective, the Moat incident emphasised the importance of police forces investing in neighbourhood policing to strengthen engagement, develop partnerships and build trust in local communities, to reduce crime and keep people safe. As the last of the police horses cantered out of Rothbury to return to the stables, and the crisp autumnal weather slowly descended on the village, normality was an abstract term, as all communities evolve as life changes over time. The Moat incident was clearly a seismic shock, and Rothbury needed time to absorb and make sense of it, but it will surely ebb away into distant memory. The outcome was fortuitous – we got away with it.

7
TRIAL

As the dust settled in the aftermath of Moat, and policing was restored to 'business as usual', the due process of criminal trials, coroners' inquests and IPCC inquiries took their course.

CRIMINAL TRIAL: R v NESS AND AWAN

Newcastle Crown Court, situated on the historic Newcastle Quayside, would determine the fate of Karl Ness and Qhuram Awan. Both had been remanded in custody, facing charges of conspiracy to commit murder, and firearms and related offences. The trial took place in January 2011.

Karl Ness, 26, of Dudley, a small former mining village on the outskirts of North Tyneside, had a close relationship with Moat. He had kept in close contact with Moat while he was in prison, and looked after his tree-surgery business. The court heard how Ness was a willing participant in planning and carrying out the shootings. He stalked the movements of Samantha Stobbart, procured the shotgun and ammunition, transported Moat to the shootings of Brown and Stobbart, and was present when PC David Rathband was shot and seriously injured in his traffic patrol car. Paul Stone QC, in defending Ness, said, 'Had it not been for Moat, none of these offences would have been committed.'

Qhuram Awan, 23, of Blyth, a coastal industrial town in Northumberland, worked as a car mechanic. Following his acquaintance with Ness and Moat, he drove the men around in his black Lexus car. When they came across PC Rathband parked up at the roundabout, Awan stopped the car, allowing Moat to creep up on the officer and shoot him twice in the face. Jeremy Carter-Manning QC, defending Awan, told the court that psychiatric tests showed his client was easily led. 'This trial is Hamlet without the prince,' he said, referring to the absence of Moat. His client remained 'horrified' by the officer's shooting, he added.

The court heard how Ness and Awan appeared calm and relaxed as they assisted Moat in buying camping supplies. They were present when Moat robbed a fish shop in Seaton Delaval and helped him set up camp at Rothbury. Although both claimed to have been held hostage, neither contacted the police. During the trial, Ness and Awan claimed they went along with Moat's demands as they were in fear for their lives and their families. Letters submitted to the court suggested otherwise. Awan wrote, 'I am actually safer than safe … burn this letter after you have read it.'

PC Trevor Weldon and I attended court and gave evidence in relation to the detention of Ness, his transport to custody and the seizure of the mobile phones found in his possession. Court security was tight and the media presence strong – live national news broadcasts were conducted from outside the court building. PC Rathband wept in the public gallery as details of the case and his injuries were read to the court by prosecuting barrister Robert Smith QC. The judge was shown a photograph of the officer's injuries as he lay in a hospital bed. Mr Smith told the court, 'The injuries rendered him blind for life. PC Rathband is still a serving police officer with Northumbria Police.' The judge replied, 'Long may he continue to be so.'

Following the five-week criminal trial, high court judge The Rt. Hon. Lord Justice McCombe summed up the case:

> You probably think it is abundantly clear that Raoul Moat murdered Chris Brown, attempted to murder PC Rathband, and robbed a fish and chip shop with a shotgun. The question is to decide whether either or both of the defendants also plotted to help. This is not a trial of Raoul Moat; it is the trial of Qhuram Awan and Karl Ness.[6]

The jury reached their verdict, with Ness convicted of the murder of Christopher Brown and possession of a firearm with intent to endanger life. Both defendants were convicted of conspiracy to murder PC Rathband, the attempted murder of PC Rathband and robbery (at the Seaton Delaval Fish Bar). Lord Justice McCombe said:

> Here we have a case where three men formulated a plan to murder policemen indiscriminately, and then, pursuant to the plan, attempted to kill one officer, with appalling consequences [...] the roles played by these two defendants cannot be minimised.

> While the offences may not have been committed without Moat, it is difficult to see that they could have been committed in the manner they were without Ness and Awan respectively [...] This too can be said to be a crime meriting punishment of the utmost severity, even though these defendants did not fire the gun.

---

6 'Summing up in trial of men accused of aiding Raoul Moat.' BBC News online (March 2011). Available from www.bbc.co.uk/news/uk-england-tyne-12689521 [Accessed Nov 2019]

> Each defendant willingly joined in a plan to commit random
> murders of police officers, knowing precisely what Moat had
> already done to Mr Brown and Miss Stobbart […] The plan
> resulted in an offence that nearly achieved the aim.

The judge ruled that Ness and Awan were a danger to the
public. Both defendants were given life sentences: Ness a minimum term of 40 years before he is eligible for release, and Awan
20 years imprisonment before discharge. There was no reaction
from Ness as he was sentenced. Awan smiled ashamedly to his
father in the public gallery as he was led away.[7]

A subsequent plea to the Court of Appeal by Ness, claiming
that his sentence was excessive, was rejected.[8] In announcing
the appeal decision, Lord Judge said that Ness had taken part
in an 'appalling catalogue of crime'. In response to the claim
that his sentence was exceptional, Lord Judge said, 'It clearly is
exceptional and we recognise that. The reality is that this was a
case of exceptionally grave crime.' The rather perplexing comments from Paul Stone QC, defending Ness, in stating that the
offences would not have been committed if it had not been for
Moat, could be rephrased: the offences would not have been
committed if it were not for the gun and cartridges procured by
Ness and the transport provided by Awan.

If you make a choice in life to kill others, live by the consequences. The sentences do not in any way convey a sense
of justice to avenge the death of Chris Brown and the serious

---

7 'Raoul Moat's henchmen jailed for life.' *The Mirror* online (March 2011). Available from www.mirror.co.uk/news/uk-news/raoul-moats-henchmen-jailed-for-life-176733 [Accessed Nov 2019]

8 'Raoul Moat accomplice loses bid to reduce jail sentence.' *The Guardian* online (December 2011). Available from www.theguardian.com/uk/2011/dec/14/raoul-moat-accomplice-loses-bid [Accessed Nov 2019]

injuries caused to Samantha Stobbart and PC David Rathband. Ness and Awan still have their lives ahead of them, albeit in a restrictive HM Prison environment. What price would Chris Brown or David Rathband have given to have those freedoms, and their families too, whose suffering at times is forgotten.

CORONER'S INQUEST: RAOUL THOMAS MOAT

A coroner's inquest into the death of Moat was held in September 2011 at Newcastle Crown Court. Evidence was given to the inquest jury by senior police commanders, negotiators, firearms officers, professional witnesses and family members. Newcastle coroner David Mitford led the court through the chronological order of events that lead to the stand-off and Moat's loss of life.

Central to the inquest was the police use of the X12-XREP Tasers, obtained by Northumbria Police and discharged at the time of Moat's death. The X12 shotgun-type Tasers were only licensed in the UK for testing purposes – the weapons had not been approved by the Home Office for operational use by UK police forces.[9] Newly promoted Chief Superintendent Jo Farrell, a Tactical Silver Commander who led the manhunt for Moat, told the inquest that the decision to use non-lethal shotgun Tasers was taken to give officers surrounding Moat a chance to bring him in alive. A Taser officer from West Yorkshire Police, named as Zulu 24, gave evidence:

> One particular thing he [Moat] did say was it was all going to end in this field tonight. Mr Moat shuffled to his feet and brought the gun from under his chin and pointed it at his temple. I thought he was going to shoot himself. [The officer

---

9 'Raoul Moat inquest: Taser "never seen before" by police.' BBC News online (September 2011). Available from www.bbc.co.uk/news/uk-england-tyne-14914425 [Accessed Nov 2019]

fired the Taser at Moat's chest.] I was aware my round had struck him. I don't think it had any effect.

Another officer fired a second Taser shot at Moat, which was believed to have missed. The metal barb projectile was later recovered from the river. A police sergeant, identified as Tango 21, told the inquest:

Moat let out a yelp. I heard a bang from Mr Moat's position and saw his head rock back violently to the left side [...] then he fell back into the long grass.

In the course of the three-week inquest, Moat's brother Angus gave evidence. He thought the police made a mistake in preventing him from speaking to his brother during the stand-off. Moat's estranged father Peter Blake, 70, who he never knew, also attended the hearing. The coroner afforded Mr Blake courtesy and respect in allowing him to give evidence in the witness box. However, the coroner would not allow him to 'theorise', restricting his witness evidence to 'of minimum relevance', bearing in mind Blake and Moat had never met. Mr Blake subsequently made a formal complaint about the coroner to the Office for Judicial Complaints (OJC). The OJC ruled that the coroner was acting within his legal powers of case management in deciding Mr Blake's evidence was irrelevant and inadmissible.

One wonders why, many times in high-profile situations, people feel the need to give prominence to themselves. A moment in the sun perhaps? A brief instance in an otherwise obscure unremarkable life where a person draws attention to themselves. Media organisations may provide such opportunities – a distinguished coroner will not.

As the Moat inquest concluded, coroner Mr David Mitford stipulated that the jury must return either a verdict of suicide or an open verdict (a legal decision that records a death but does not state its cause). The coroner stipulated five questions the jury must consider:

1. Did the firing of the Taser cause Moat to shoot himself when he otherwise would not have done so?
2. Were the instructions to firearms officers appropriate?
3. Was it right to fire the Tasers?
4. Was the decision not to use Moat's half-brother Angus or his friend […] in direct negotiation appropriate?
5. Was a senior officer's decision to use Tasers appropriate?[10]

Following due deliberation, the jury returned a unanimous verdict of suicide. The jury also determined: 'At no point did Mr Moat ask to talk to any family member or friend.' The coroner thanked the jurors for their 'extremely well put-together' narrative.

INDEPENDENT POLICE COMPLAINTS COMMISSION INVESTIGATION

There was clearly some overlap between the coroner's inquest into the death of Moat and the IPCC inquiry, which focused on two specific areas of examination: the acquisition, use, authorisation and deployment of the XREP Tasers; and the prison warning notification and actions taken by Northumbria Police, when Moat threatened harm on release from prison.

The IPCC investigation in relation to the use of the XREP

10 'Raoul Moat inquest: jury considers verdict.' *The Guardian* online (September 2011). Available from www.theguardian.com/uk/2011/sep/27/raoul-moat-inquest [Accessed Nov 2019]

Taser absolved police officers of any wrongdoing. 'It is clear from the evidence that there is no suggestion any discharge from the XREP Tasers caused Moat to inadvertently pull the trigger,' IPCC Commissioner Nicholas Long said. The report found police had acted with humanity, with a well-thought-out policy of how negotiations were to be conducted, working tirelessly to avert a fatal outcome. The IPCC report author concluded there was a clear rationale for using unauthorised Tasers, for which the force sought legal advice: Mr Long said:

> I fully recognise that within such a dynamic and fast-moving operation, decisions have to be made that don't always comply with recognised policies and procedures. The force believed their intention to use whatever means they had to try to capture Moat alive, overrode any questions of authorisation.[11]

Moat was struck with a glancing blow from the Taser discharge, with little effect. The evidence showed a further distinct bodily movement to raise the shotgun to his head before he fired the fatal shot. The report acknowledged it was not realistic to remove officers from the scene to train them in the use of the Taser.

An area of criticism concerned the final moments of Moat's life, which were recorded with a hand-held recording device. 'Better and more durable equipment should have been used, and the fact it wasn't meant the opportunity to capture vital evidence in the final stages of Moat's life was lost,' the report said. One would have thought that in the planning of a potential

---

11 'IPCC probe clears Raoul Moat Taser police of misconduct.' BBC News online (September 2011). Available from www.bbc.co.uk/news/uk-england-tyne-15078301 [Accessed Nov 2019]

stand-off situation (for which specialist negotiators rehearsed in advance), the capturing of scene evidence in anticipation of legal scrutiny would have been a consideration. Force technical support officers would have been readily available to assist.

The decision by Northumbria Police Assistant Chief Constable Steve Ashman to requisition the XREP Tasers for use by officers, as a last resort to save Moat's life, was strong dynamic police leadership. Many chief officers would not have had the bottle to take a decision to use weapons that were still under testing and unauthorised by the Home Office for operational use. The rationale for the use of the weapon was also supported by the coroner during the Moat inquest. The fact that the weapon did not achieve the desired effect, while disappointing, is rather superficial. In my view, the decision by Northumbria Police was commendable.

A point worthy of note is that the Home Office implied that Northumbria Police could use the XREP Tasers during the Moat incident at their discretion, in reasonable and proportionate circumstances. It was rather unfortunate that the Home Secretary Theresa May showed a complete lack of bottle in the aftermath of the Moat incident. The XREP Taser company, Pro-Tect Systems, had its licence revoked by the Home Office for supplying an unlicensed weapon and ammunition to Northumbria Police, in breach of its terms of agreement. As a result, Pro-Tect Systems, the only supplier of Tasers in the UK, was unable to import or sell the devices: a move which would lead to fatal consequences for the company.

The IPCC findings concerning the prison notification to Northumbria Police and actions taken by the force took a different tone. Moat had told another inmate that he planned to take revenge on those who had wronged him. The IPCC expressed concerns at the reluctance by Northumbria Police to act on the intelligence, correctly passed to the force's Domestic Violence Unit by prison authorities. IPCC Commissioner Cindy Butts said it was 'unsatisfactory' that two police officers had failed to act on intelligence, and that Moat, on his release from prison, was a danger to the public:

> He specifically named Samantha Stobbart on his list of targets, and made reference to a new boyfriend [...]
>
> Instead, the officers finished their shift knowing that a woman may be at risk of assault. Considering the focus of the role filled by both officers in the Domestic Violence Unit must be to provide reassurance and protection to vulnerable people, their failure to act on intelligence was frankly unbelievable.[12]

Northumbria Police's now Deputy Chief Constable Steve Ashman denied the allegations. He said the IPCC report was 'flawed' and its conclusions were 'grossly unfair and inconsistent' with the official findings of coroner Mr Terence Carney on the death of Christopher Brown, who was shot within two days of Moat's release from prison. During the inquest into Christopher Brown's death, held at Newcastle Crown Court, Mr Carney highlighted failures by the prison service and Northumbria Police; however, he concluded that any failures had not 'directly' caused the death of Brown. 'We got tantalisingly close to a point of the information being actually known, as opposed

---

12 'Police under fire for handling of Raoul Moat manhunt in 2010.' *Independent* online (January 2014) Accessible from www.independent.co.uk/news/uk/crime/police-under-fire-for-handling-of-raoul-moat-manhunt-in-2010-9039177.html [Accessed Nov 2019]

to speculatively known,' he said.[13] The inquest found that Christopher Brown was unlawfully killed by Raoul Moat. Deputy Chief Constable Ashman defended the force, stating:

> It is regrettable that the IPCC Commissioner has chosen to make emotive comments about this tragic matter in the context of an IPCC investigation which was flawed, and an inquest [into the death of Christopher Brown] which the commissioner did not attend.

With emotions clearly tetchy on both sides, an examination of the IPCC draft report in 2012 may shed some light. In a conversation with a fellow inmate, Moat had made specific threats to shoot a number of people, including Samantha Stobbart and her new boyfriend [Chris Brown]. The inmate passed the information to a prison officer but could not remember the exact words used by Moat. Apparently, the inmate watered down the nature of the intelligence, from serious threats to life to a threat of serious harm. A prison officer completed a Security Information Report, documenting that Moat intended to 'seriously assault' his partner. Over the next 24 hours the information report was passed between various prison in-trays, having been read by senior prison officers.

On the afternoon of Friday, 2 July, the day after Moat's release from prison, a Durham Prison probation officer passed the intelligence by telephone to Northumbria Police's Public Protection Unit, which included specialist domestic violence officers. The IPCC report stated that a perceived conflict with police records, regarding details of the identity of Moat's partner, appeared to

---

13 'Coroner rules precise risk posed by Raoul Moat was not known.' *The Chronicle* Live online (December 2013). Available from www.chroniclelive.co.uk/news/chris-brown-inquest-coroner-rules-6396133 [Accessed Nov 2019]

have frustrated any possibility of intelligence being pursued with further police action. What remained unanswered was a threat by Raoul Moat that he was going to seriously harm his partner, whoever that proved to be. The intelligence was also emailed to the Northumbria Police Force Intelligence Bureau (FIB) at 4:15 pm on the Friday, but staff had apparently gone home at 4:00 pm. Within 11 hours Christopher Brown was shot dead and his ex-partner Samantha Stobbart seriously wounded.[14]

While the IPCC said there was no evidence of misconduct by the two police officers, their failure to follow procedures regarding a threat of domestic violence was considered to be a performance issue. A senior Northumbria Police officer said the information was not specific and was treated in the same way as they would have done with any report. 'To try and suggest that we could have prevented that I think is a step too far. I am convinced he would have done what he intended doing, such was his focus,' he said. As a consequence of the IPCC inquiry, the force introduced changes at the FIB so that it operated around the clock.

On reflection, the threat from Moat to cause serious harm following his prison release, as communicated from HMP Durham to Northumbria Police, may have been imprecise and its dissemination from Durham Prison to Northumbria Police unjustifiably delayed. However, Northumbria Police had a duty to act on the information, to negate the threat to cause serious harm, and to safeguard any potential victims.

I acknowledge that hindsight is a wonderful thing and

---

14 'Raoul Moat threat not acted upon by police or prison.' BBC News online (April 2012) Available from www.bbc.co.uk/news/uk-england-tyne-17840610 [Accessed Nov 2019]

numerous such threats are made by members of the prison population on a regular basis. The fact the information was of sufficient concern to be escalated by phone and email by prison authorities should have triggered a police response and not been passively dismissed, as implied in the IPCC report. Reading between the lines, the chances of gaining the full attention of any police headquarters department staff after 4:00 pm on a Friday always presented difficulties, with most having gone home for the weekend. The term 'poets' day is not used without good reason: 'Piss Off Early, Tomorrow's Saturday'.

Even though the threat of serious harm may have been imprecise, and specialist domestic violence officers unavailable for whatever reason, the intelligence could have been referred to an on-duty neighbourhood sergeant covering the area of Moat's address, if partner details had not yet been ascertained. One of the main roles of a neighbourhood sergeant is to oversee safeguarding in their local community. Neighbourhood officers routinely develop information and community intelligence, liaise with duty social services, conduct welfare checks with victims and vulnerable people and determine if there are safeguarding concerns. Neighbourhood sergeants are specialised in developing safeguarding plans and putting in place interventions, enacted by local officers, to protect members of their community – the primary duty of the police.

The force, in asserting that the coroner at the inquest of Christopher Brown did not attribute the prison–police intelligence inaction 'directly' to the cause of his death, does not entirely negate the IPCC report. Hanging your hat on the conclusion of the coroner may present credibility; however, what appears a more in-depth forensic examination of this issue by the IPCC should not be readily discounted. As an analogy, a mechanic who does not repair the brakes on a bus, which results in a fatal collision, may not be *directly* responsible for the crash, but they, by their inaction, may have indirectly contributed to, or failed to prevent, the injuries or death.

It was surely not beyond the capabilities of Northumbria Police to develop the imprecise prison information, identify the individuals closely connected to Moat, and then establish if the threat was credible or believed, and implement appropriate safeguarding measures to protect any person deemed at risk. The information from the prison service, whether a threat to life or potential cause of serious harm, was rather marginal and immaterial. That said, Northumbria Police did not have a crystal ball to predict a man would acquire a firearm and use the weapon to deadly effect. Even if the force had gone the full mile to address safeguarding and security measures for Samantha Stobbart and Chris Brown, who were both aware of Moat's threats of violence, a raging, single-minded Moat would have been nigh-on impossible to stop.

CRIMINAL JUSTICE SYSTEM

One aspect barely touched on was the wider failings of the criminal justice system. Short sentences, no offender supervision for sentences under 12 months and early prisoner release make a mockery of the original court sentence imposed. If longer sentences were given and early prison release curtailed, with intensive offender management programmes by the probation services, the community would be better protected and the victim population significantly reduced. Public trust would improve in what is otherwise a failing criminal justice system.

Moat was released with no probation supervision after serving around half of an 18-week prison sentence for assault on a child. If a more robust approach had been adopted, the death and serious injuries caused to others – and his own suicide – may have been prevented.

The costs to society of not investing in the criminal justice system and, instead, systematically dismantling the government agencies and institutions involved, as well as local community services, has taken a severe toll on the British public. Under the tenure of The Right Honourable Theresa May, first as Home Secretary and then as Prime Minister, crime has significantly increased, with persistent offenders committing crimes at will, resulting in victims who should not have been victims and causing deaths that could have been prevented.

CIVIL COURT CASE: DAVID RATHBAND AND THE CHIEF CONSTABLE OF THE NORTHUMBRIA CONSTABULARY

Following the conclusion of criminal proceedings, coroners' inquests and IPCC investigations, a further court process began in January 2016, instigated by PC David Rathband: civil action against the Chief Constable of Northumbria Police.

The claimant stated that Northumbria Police owed PC Rathband a duty of care to warn him of the threats made by Moat, and they were negligent in failing to issue an immediate warning. If issued, PC Rathband would not have been a sitting duck, it was alleged. Central to the case was the 999 call made by Moat to Northumbria Police in which he said, 'I am hunting for officers now …' Several minutes later, PC Rathband was shot at close range, resulting in horrific injuries and the loss of his sight, which led to the breakdown of his marriage and his unexpected tragic death in February 2012. The continuance of this civil action was taken up by his sister, Debbie Essery, and twin brother Darren Rathband. Notably, his wife did not take part.

Court submissions claimed the officer in charge of the operation, then Superintendent Joanna Farrell, was negligent in failing to give immediate instructions for an interim warning to be issued. The defendant, the Chief Constable of Northumbria Police, who was vicariously liable for the actions of his officers, denied the claim. Both sides produced former senior police officers as expert witnesses during the eight-day hearing at the High Court of Justice.

The court heard how Northumbria Police conducted a threat assessment following the killing of Chris Brown and the shooting of Samantha Stobbart. Moat had threatened to kill a number of named individuals in addition to Stobbart and Brown; all were connected to him in some way, none were police officers. Northumbria Police took steps to notify and protect those individuals deemed at risk, with firearms officers deployed in support.

Moat's 999 call to Northumbria Police at 00:29 am on Sunday, 4 July, lasted nearly five minutes and included several significant statements: his determination he would not be taken alive; a threat to kill police officers if they came near him; a claim to have two hostages; and a threat, not merely to kill police officers, but to actively seek them out: 'I'm coming to get yous, I'm not on the run I am coming to get you.' Around nine minutes after the call ended, PC Rathband was shot.

During the call, the control room supervision took immediate steps to trace Moat's location. Meanwhile, the Communications

Critical Incident Manager, of inspector rank, notified the Tactical Firearms Commander, Superintendent Jo Farrell. Coordinates supplied to police on receipt of the 999 call showed the caller's location to the west and south of Gateshead. Further examination of the call data, had it been undertaken, would have shown a larger area where the call was made, which included the roundabout in Newcastle where PC Rathband was static in his patrol car. Specialist police telecoms staff conducted cell-site analysis with the telecoms provider to identify the specific phone masts used, to try to pinpoint the caller's location.

Superintendent Farrell, an experienced firearms and critical incident commander, awaited the result of the cell-site analysis as the information would provide a better indication of Moat's location, whether he was on foot or in a vehicle and his direction of travel. (The subsequent result identified a possible 200-square-kilometre area to the north-west of Newcastle, which was of little use.) An email recording of the emergency call from Moat was forwarded to Superintendent Farrell, who was based at Newcastle North Police Station. In listening to the call, the senior officer would be able to make a more informed threat assessment in deciding actions to protect individuals and police officers and to trace Moat.

While the Communications Critical Incident Manager had authority to broadcast an urgent radio warning to patrolling officers, this would have been highly unusual without consulting Superintendent Farrell, who had specific responsibility for the police operation to locate Moat. Before a threat assessment of the call could be made, or an urgent police radio warning transmitted, PC Rathband was shot at 00:44 am.

Following the incident, a police warning was broadcast

shortly before 00:55 am for all unarmed officers in the Newcastle and Gateshead area to return to their police stations. With one officer shot and others believed to be in immediate danger, this was a drastic step to take. The direction left a limited police presence on the streets during the early hours of a busy weekend, which affected their ability to provide an effective service for the protection of the public.

Mr Justice Males, who presided over the civil case brought by David Rathband, referred to a management review by Northumbria Police of the handling of events by the force Communications department. Chief Superintendent Gordon Milward conducted the review, and his first draft concluded:

> It was not possible to develop a response to Moat's threats and communicate it concisely [to patrolling officers] in the time between the call and the assault on PC Rathband ...

Chief Constable Sue Sim did not agree; her view was that it would have been possible to issue some sort of warning, and she required the report to be changed. The final version concluded:

> It was not possible to develop an all-encompassing, fully risk-assessed response to Moat's threats and communicate it concisely in the time between the call and the assault on PC Rathband, however a more immediate, interim warning could have been given by the CIM [Critical Incident Manager] whilst the full response was being devised in conjunction with the TFC [Tactical Firearms Commander], Superintendent Farrell.

In my view, any interference in the findings of any internal report seriously undermines its authenticity. The revised 'flowery' version appears to appease the chief constable, protect the superintendent and apportion criticism at the lower-ranking critical incident manager. Perhaps Chief Constable Sim did not fully appreciate the Communications room dynamics involved in making such operational real-time critical decisions. In his judgment, Mr Justice Males appeared rather dismissive of the report, stating that it was clear this report was written with the benefit of hindsight and would have been written differently if, for example, an officer had been shot while on foot patrol in Newcastle city centre.

Following Northumbria Police's management review report, recommendations were made to amend the force's safe-patrolling procedures, including guidance if a similar situation were to take place:

- the threat is broadcast at the earliest opportunity to front-line staff
- no foot patrols
- double crewing
- avoid static positions when on patrol
- remain mobile or return to the police station.

The revised safe-patrolling procedures appeared to be the only significant actions implemented for front-line officers following the Moat incident.

Mr Justice Males, in his closing judgment, concluded that the civil claim must fail:

> It is well-established law that in making operational decisions concerning the investigation and suppression of crime, particularly when such decisions have to be made under pressure of time, the police do not owe a private law duty of care either to members of the public or to police officers.[15]

15 Mr Justice Males. 2016. *David Rathband and the Chief Constable of the Northumbria Constabulary:* High Court of Justice Queen's Bench Division Newcastle District Registry Case No: HQ12X00232. Available from https://www.judiciary.uk/wp-content/uploads/2016/02/rathband-v-northumbria-police.pdf [Accessed Nov 2019]

The judgment's clear and unequivocal findings concluded that Superintendent Farrell was not negligent; she had only three-and-a-half minutes in which to do anything that would have averted the shooting. 'In all probability that was simply not enough time,' the judge said. Unless PC Rathband had moved off almost instantaneously, a warning would not have averted his shooting. 'I am not persuaded that he would have done so.'

Mr Justice Males referred to the emotion that PC Rathband described in his book, in contemplating the likelihood that if it had not been him who was shot, it would have been one of his fellow officers:

> It could have been any of us. My pride tells me that I stopped one of my mates getting shot and who knows how many members of the public. He could have gone into the city centre, pretending to ask for directions, and blown any cop's face off when they wound down the window. Or turned up at the police station and done the same. Imagine that happening to a female colleague of yours in her twenties and having to explain it to her parents or young baby. I have to believe that I took one for my colleagues.
>
> —*Tango 190: The David Rathband Story*[16]

The judge stated that PC Rathband's bleak assessment was probably right. He was desperately unlucky to be the victim of Moat's cruelty and hatred, but if it had not been him it would probably have been somebody else.

Northumbria Police would have taken no comfort in the outcome of the civil case, following their robust defence to the claim the officer was let down by the force. Welfare support to

---

16 *Tango 190: The David Rathband Story*. David Rathband (April 2012)

the officer was of the highest level, with the provision of finance, private health care, a medical pension if he wished, no money to be taken from criminal injury settlements, and a job kept open in the Roads Policing Unit if he wanted to return to duty.

No one can imagine the suffering David was going through – the loss of his sight bringing loneliness and isolation, being unable to see his children and family, and the pain, anger, depression and growing mistrust of others. Above all, he must have thought, *Why me?* David's fight and bravery, in coming to terms with his severe injuries and blindness, led him to establish the Blue Lamp Foundation, a charity he founded to support ambulance, police and fire personnel injured in the course of duty; it was an immense achievement, which speaks volumes about the man David Rathband was.

Sadly, as the judgment reflects, David appeared to have been under the impression that there was a much greater delay between the threats from Moat being received and carried out – a belief that suggestions were made at the time that a warning should be issued but that they were fobbed off. A cock-up and cover-up by the force. An organisation that he had been so proud to serve had let him down. Clearly, after detailed legal scrutiny, this was not the case. As Mr Justice Males concluded, one of the many sad aspects of this case was that PC Rathband died under this mistaken impression.

The civil case of Rathband against the Chief Constable of Northumbria Police was concluded in February 2016, ending a period of more than five years of trials and inquiries into the carnage inflicted by one man – Raoul Thomas Moat. And at what cost? In terms of policing, courts, hospitals and prisons, and in jailing Ness and Awan for at least 60 years? Tens of millions of pounds spent on one man's mission of selfish revenge. What about the human costs – to the victims, their families and communities, all bearing the brunt of Moat's calling.

What of prime ministers, chancellors, and ministers of state for the Home Office and the Ministry of Justice, all responsible for the criminal justice system? All accountable for a lack of investment in the police, courts, prisons, probation and support services, and their failure to have a coherent plan to address the disconnect between the various criminal justice institutions. Is it not the first duty of any sovereign parliament to protect its citizens?

Maybe the significant sum of money needed to be invested in a longer-term approach was not politically expedient, in the shorter term, to attribute any significant electoral gain. The criminal justice system was a significant factor in failing to protect Moat's victims, as is the case with thousands of victims of crime each year. The trials, inquiries and inquests simply mop up the water, where there is a need to turn off the tap.

8
MEDIA
MADNESS

The next lie I see in the paper, I'm going to kill an innocent member of the public.

These chilling words of intent from Raoul Moat were in response to tabloid media reporting that he perceived to be lies. Media coverage of the police hunt for Moat, leading to his death, has been subject to widespread criticism. To what extent did the media influence the event? What was the effect on Northumbria Police? More broadly, who determines what is in the public interest? Do the media bear any responsibility for the outcome?

Without question there was a legitimate media and public interest in the reporting of an armed gunman who presented a danger to the community. Moat had killed a man, seriously injured his ex-partner and shot a police officer. There was an unrelenting need for information to satisfy the demands of 24-hour news coverage. Competing newspaper, broadcast and internet organisations fought to capture public attention and market share, and the boundaries of responsible, informative journalism at times gave way to sensationalism and dramatic eye-catching headlines, giving Moat cult status and ending in his death, captured live on television.

The relationship between the media and police was never

going to be easy. After the shooting of Chris Brown and Moat's ex-partner Samantha Stobbart in Birtley, the initial media response was mainly confined to a regional reporting level. Following the attempted murder of PC David Rathband, interest from the national press gathered momentum. An armed and dangerous killer at large bore comparison to the shooting incident in Cumbria a few weeks before, when 12 people were shot dead by taxi driver Derrick Bird: an incident of incredible rarity in the United Kingdom.

Northumbria Police media department arranged daily news conferences, attended by Temporary Chief Constable Sue Sim and Head of Crime, Detective Chief Superintendent Neil Adamson. Strong and trusted mutual working relationships were already established between the force and regional media organisations. The initial police–media strategy was to inform and reassure the public as police enquiries continued to locate and safely apprehend Moat.

Northumbria Police News Conference – Sunday, 4 July 2010

I would like to start by offering my sincere condolences and sympathy to family and friends of those that have been killed and injured [...] At quarter to one this morning, a uniform motor patrols officer [...] was approached by an armed man and shot. The officer suffered a gunshot wound and was taken to hospital [...] His condition is described as critical but stable at this time. The injured officer is PC David Rathband.

We are absolutely committed to finding the man who did this [...] We now know this shooting is linked to the incident in Gateshead [...] where a man was killed and a woman seriously injured.

The man we are looking for is Raoul Thomas Moat [...]

I want to reassure the public that everything is being done to locate Moat. I also want to stress, that the safety of the public and our staff is our absolute priority [...]
—*T/Chief Constable Sue Sim*

Northumbria Police news conferences were not too dissimilar to those held following domestic-related murders. Senior officers provided the latest investigation update, key reassurance messages were emphasised and public information requests made. In the case of Moat, the suspect was known to police; however, his whereabouts, associates and the vehicle he was using were unknown. CCTV footage seized from PC David Rathband's patrol car assisted in the identification of the black Lexus saloon car that Moat was using in the company of his mate Karl Ness and Qhuram Awan. The vehicle details were released to the media, with information sought from the public on any sightings.

A spanner in the works was the call to Northumbria Police from Raoul Moat, where he stated he had taken two hostages. Senior investigating officers, while having their misgivings, dealt with the hostage report in accordance with national guidelines on kidnap. A news blackout was requested of all media organisations in relation to the hostages, on the grounds that there was a potential risk to life which could not be negated: a specific police request made privately to the media before the main Northumbria Police press conference. All media organisations willingly complied, which reflected the collective trust and goodwill shown in those early days of the investigation.

Northumbria Police's Media Department was well resourced. Almost 40 media staff were employed to protect a strong organisational reputation and public brand. In any criminal investigation, effective media communications are widely acknowledged as essential. During the early stages of the Moat incident, the force praised the media and public for their support. Moat's grievance was initially directed towards the police and those in authority, not the general public. Northumbria Police urgently sought information on his whereabouts. Moat was believed to have access to mobile smartphones, which led to a direct appeal from senior officers.

Northumbria Police News Conference – Monday, 5 July 2010

Our thoughts remain with the family and friends of those who have been killed and injured at this difficult time. We remain absolutely committed to finding Raoul Thomas Moat and are using every resource available to bring this to a conclusion as quickly as possible [...] The vitally important issue now, is the safety of the public and our efforts to secure that, by finding Mr Moat [...] The support of yourselves the media, and the public has been invaluable to us so far. I would like to thank you for that, and ask that your continued help in this challenging and fast-moving investigation be provided [...]
—*T/Chief Constable Sue Sim*

I want to reiterate my appeal [...] Mr Moat. We are aware you have a number of issues and grievances [...] We want to understand your position and I want you to realise that you do have a future [...] We've spoken to Sam [Stobbart] and she has asked us to say the following to you: 'Please give yourself up. If you still loved me and our baby you would not be doing this anymore [...] I have not been seeing a police officer.'

Mr Moat, [...] please make contact with us [...]
—*Detective Chief Superintendent Neil Adamson*

Overnight, the Moat incident became national headlines across all television networks, newspapers and online platforms. At the time, there appeared no other substantive newsworthy stories or events of significance taking place. No doubt the metropolitan-based news organisations had purchased maps and requisitioned staff in readiness for their dispatch to North East England.

With the discovery of the black Lexus abandoned at an industrial estate in Rothbury, firearms officers swooped on the peaceful Northumberland rural village in the hunt for Moat. The two reported 'hostages' were safely located, walking away from Rothbury, and both were arrested by police using hard-stop techniques of military precision. Clearly they were hostages no more.

Northumbria Police were delighted with the breakthrough, and confident it was only a matter of time before Moat would be found. Relations with the media had been encouraging, with the hostage news blackout fully respected. However, senior officers had real concerns about the media entourage travelling en masse and smothering a quiet rural village.

Northumbria Police News Conference – Tuesday, 6 July 2010

Late yesterday afternoon, I asked for the cooperation and assistance of the media. I asked you not to release specific information which if released could have caused a significant threat to life in relation to this enquiry. Can I thank you for your support with this request [...]

Shortly after 10:00 am this morning [...] we arrested two men who were on foot walking along a public road in Rothbury, Northumberland. I can confirm that both men are the people we believe were the hostages. Both have been arrested on suspicion of conspiracy to commit murder [...]

At this time Mr Moat has not been located. I am confident, however, with the support of the wider public and the continuing efforts of our staff we are closing the net on Moat […]

It will serve no purpose and indeed hinder our efforts should the mass media descend upon what is a small rural Northumberland village. I strongly urge you not to travel to the area […]

—*Chief Superintendent Neil Adamson*

Following the imposition of a two-mile ground exclusion zone and vehicle checkpoints around Rothbury, residents were advised to stay indoors for their protection. The lockdown was further strengthened, by a five-mile air exclusion zone. As a sign of things to come, the air exclusion zone was immediately breached by a light aircraft, believed to have been chartered by members of the press.

Hopeful pleas to dissuade the mass media from attending Rothbury appeared to fall on deaf ears, as journalists and broadcasters left the comfort of their metropolis-based studios on a summer jaunt, up to the unspoiled Northumberland countryside. With Moat having gone to ground, literally scores of journalists, camera crews, television engineers and producers swooped on the village as the media circus rolled into town.

All available hotel and guest house accommodation was fully booked. Media gazebos and pop-up tents were pitched on any accessible public space in the village, accompanied by satellite broadcast vans and media industry personnel. Local reporters and regional broadcasters also gathered to conduct interviews with local people; however, one got the impression they had been edged aside as the status of the larger media beasts took centre stage. Prime-time news presenters from Sky, BBC, ITN and other media organisations arrived on location, to the bemusement of some residents.

Locally trusted news organisations, such as BBC Look North, ITV Tyne Tees, the *Newcastle Chronicle* and the *Northumberland Gazette* had, over many years, earned the respect of Northumberland communities. They would be reporting local news long after the Moat incident was consigned to history. Many national television networks, newspapers and agencies were unlikely to ever return to Rothbury; hence, their feelings towards the local community were secondary to pursuing immediate journalistic demands.

The media's agenda was now driven by the national press, with headlines describing Moat as 'Britain's Most Wanted Man'. As the police manhunt became protracted over several days, gaps in media content were filled by probing Moat's mental state and his muscular physique, which, it was claimed, was a result of steroid abuse. Newspaper headlines and some of the terminology used were more akin to a Hollywood action movie, as if to elevate his box-office appeal, depicting masculinity and violence: 'Mohican Murderer' and 'Psycho Commando'.

Despite the best efforts of reporters to portray the people of Rothbury as scared and in a panic, residents presented to the contrary – they were a little tense but otherwise unfazed. Several residents were appalled by reporters hiding in gardens and asking leading questions, in seeking to cultivate dramatic headlines. A local farmer was asked, 'You're going to arm yourself with your gun to protect your family?' to which he replied, 'No, not really, I have every confidence in the police.' One local parish councillor expressed his concerns at the attitude, behaviour and writings of the press. He described them as 'behaving like vultures'.

Instead of the media content being driven by specialist firearms units in action, or high-octane police pursuits, coverage had to contend with a more sedate and charming rural village way of life: armed police on foot patrol, engaging warmly with the local butcher, baker and candlestick maker; and children, seemingly without a care in the world, walking to school accompanied by parents. Content gaps in television news programmes were filled with so-called experts who explained how to survive in the wild, what to eat, how to take shelter and where to hide (derelict buildings, forests and caves). Unwittingly, they may have provided support to an eavesdropping Raoul Moat. When a TV bushcraft presenter found an abandoned plastic carrier bag during a search of woodland, even that was elevated to a possible critical lead as to Moat's whereabouts. Descriptions of firearms and demonstrations of police weaponry also filled broadcasting time and maybe raised the testosterone levels of some excitable television viewers. As the days passed, there was still no trace of Moat.

Northumbria Police attempted to keep media organisations on board by inviting them to a live search operation near the riverbank, in the area of Beggars Rigg car park, just outside the village. The search, by all accounts, was simulated – staged for the media. The specialist search officers involved were frustrated with senior officers for diverting scarce police resources to perform a search for the benefit of the press, when actually looking for Moat was the priority. Therein lies the impression that, for all the vast media police assets, the experience of the force was limited in handling the intrusive demands of the national media.

Press coverage began to adopt a more sinister approach. Media scrutiny and newspaper headlines turned to Moat's dysfunctional family, his previous relationships and derogatory interpretations of his childhood past:

'Cute baby but two-month-old baby clenches his fist.'

'At five his eyes already have an intense look.'

'YOU'RE BETTER OFF DEAD SON' (And that's Moat's mother speaking)

'I WILL KILL YOU MAM' – The angelic boy who became a monster

Perhaps the media organisations concerned would care to explain why inflammatory details were printed that had no conceivable justification of being in the public interest. The derogatory media coverage, predominantly in the tabloid press, had not gone unnoticed by Moat, who recorded a dictaphone message threatening to kill an innocent member of the public for each lie published.

Northumbria Police held a press briefing, where Moat's threat to the public was revealed. Afterwards, police convened a private meeting with the media to request confidentiality concerning Moat's threat to harm the community and to seek their restraint in making personal attacks. The force should have convened the confidential meeting first, followed by the open press briefing, similar to the hostage news blackout appeal. In essence, attempting to close the door after the horse had bolted led to information that was intended to be confidential being publicly disclosed by the media. Whatever the communications breakdown, it was apparent that police relations with some elements of the media were at breaking point.

Northumbria Police News Conference – Thursday, 8 July 2010

I am aware that this enquiry is now entering its sixth day
[…] From the outset we have stressed Mr Moat's grievances
are largely directed towards the police. Information has now
emerged that Mr Moat has made threats towards the wider
public […] My officers are out in large numbers to provide
reassurance and protection […]

Finally, I would like to appeal to everyone – the public
and the media – for their continued patience and ask that
my officers are given the space they need to carry out their
duties without being hindered.

T/Chief Constable Sue Sim

Further exacerbating any hope of an *entente cordiale* between
police and sections of the media was the reference to Moat
being a 'nutter' by Inspector Sue Peart. Unfortunately, the use
of the term was an open goal for the media to criticise police for
using such inflammatory language, which the force had specifically requested the media to avoid. Clearly there was impatience
building from elements of the press, as the days passed by without any tangible progress in finding Moat.

A barrage of personal attacks from the press were aimed at
T/Chief Constable Sue Sim, who had become the public face
of Northumbria Police. Hurtful comments were directed at her
appearance, with unflattering nicknames and mocking comparisons made with television characters. Minor slip-ups at press
conferences were also ridiculed, despite local people in Rothbury
having immense trust and confidence in their chief constable,
which was soon vindicated in Moat's discovery by the riverbank
on the Friday evening.

As Moat lay motionless on the grass, pointing a gun to his

head, police attempted to secure the scene as a media frenzy erupted, with reporters scrambling towards Riverside to seek a closer view, despite a risk to their safety and police directions to move back behind cordons. An impromptu gathering of reporters and local people took to the main street as the live situation unfolded. On the High Street, near to where Moat was contained, unscripted live television interviews took place between news presenters and residents. Police officers attempted to push back the gathering crowd to create a safe, sterile area. A visibly distressed female resident, surrounded by reporters and camera crews, expressed concerns for her mother, who was confined to her home near the scene. During a live television broadcast, the resident was asked by a reporter of national repute to contact her mother and put her mobile phone on audio speaker, to allow her mother's response to be heard – live on national television. The daughter glared at the media correspondent. 'That's a bit impersonal.'

Reporters scrambled to advantageous positions surrounding the riverbank – they hid behind trees and lurked in bushes to gain a ringside seat. That exclusive photograph or recording of the live stand-off was a once-in-a-lifetime career opportunity that was too good to miss. Attempts by local officers to direct reporters away from the scene were at times fruitless, leaving one police officer visibly shaken. Photographers shouted, 'Look this way, Raoul,' which severely hampered police attempts to secure the area and calm the situation. Several reporters displayed an air of invincibility, with scant regard for Moat's volatility and his loathing of the media, as if they had a press pass which exempted them from harm.

As darkness fell, and heavy rainfall dampened the illuminated scene, police negotiations continued throughout the night in the hope of securing a peaceful resolution. Instead of live 24/7 news broadcasts humanely pulling away from coverage – to show less intrusion and greater dignity – as the right thing to do, coverage went into overdrive. Earlier footage of Moat's discovery and the reaction of residents was repeated on a continuous loop, blended with impromptu analysis as to how the situation would play out. Television viewers were transfixed, held in anticipation. Would he live, or would he die?

Without warning, the uncanny silence was shattered, with the sound of gunshots and raised voices as police charged towards Moat. The media coverage reached a climax as action from the scene was broadcast live across the nation as the final moments of the seven-day manhunt unfolded. The fatally injured Moat was rushed to hospital by ambulance, where his death was confirmed shortly after arrival – television at its most dynamic.

There has been a great deal of debate about the way Moat's death was beamed live across the UK's media and beyond. His brother Angus was highly critical, stating he was probably the only person to ever witness his own brother die live on national television. The ending of Moat's life brings into question how to cover an active criminal event played out live on television and online. Psychologists question whether the media coverage had the power to encourage or, indirectly, contribute to Moat pulling the trigger.

The media's role in the Raoul Moat incident has been the subject of endless discussion and argument. While the Moat incident may not go down in history as Fleet Street's finest hour, the implication that journalists as a whole were overly intrusive, too inquisitive and obstructive to police, would not be accurate or fair. Media reporting and content, by the many respected journalists, was highly professional, informative, factual, supportive to police and not in any way sensationalised.

Sadly, events in UK journalism from 2007 led to the rise of minority elements of the feral media, to the detriment of the vast majority of genuine, decent, hard-working industry professionals. Despicable acts of unlawful behaviour, culture, practices and ethics, including phone-hacking, were identified in the Leveson Inquiry, with the final report published November 2012.

While press accountability may have improved following the Leveson Inquiry, the failure of respective governments to act fully on Lord Justice Leveson's recommendations speaks volumes about our parliamentary standards, at times overly beholden to powerful press barons to the perceived disadvantage of individual citizens. Trial by media and the intrusion into people's personal and family lives is still prevalent, and the genuine public interest for doing so questionable. The need to further regulate the press and online content, including fake news, must be a work in progress, notwithstanding the need to protect fundamental human rights and safeguard press freedoms, underpinning a free and democratic society.

On reflection, Northumbria Police were at times overwhelmed by the power of the media and the 24/7 live news environment. In all honesty, could any other police force have fared much better with the insatiable demands for real-time content, an urge for sensationalism, biased impressions of news events, and the truth being influenced by interpretation, rather than sound ethical principles of impartiality?

Senior investigation officers would have learned a great deal from the Moat episode. Police were deeply concerned that the conduct of some elements of the media were negatively impacting on the investigation and the safety of the community; notwithstanding, police are not averse to advancing their own angle of focus in shaping events. Unfortunately, whatever the force media strategy was, it was unlikely to satisfy the demands of the dog-eat-dog news industry, fighting for its very own survival. A possible way forward in such events would be to formalise an agreed memorandum of understanding in advance, between police and the attending media organisations, underpinned by broadcasting and press regulatory bodies. This would serve to improve relations, build trust, and formalise agreed news blackouts at times of sensitivity or immediate risk to life.

Ultimately, does the consumer of news also play a part in driving the content? The public demand for gratifying, sensationalised content in real time helps to feed the media machine.[17] Moat's fate was played out on live television, with viewers experiencing a human instinct to look and a feeling of guilt in watching, but despite this there was still a reluctance to change channels. Perhaps, indirectly, we are all part of this madness, with the exception of Rothbury residents, who remained dignified and resolute throughout, placing their trust in Northumbria Police and each other. The force privately acknowledges that if this manhunt had occurred in a 'non-idyllic' urban centre of population then the natives would likely have become restless, inflamed by the media, adding a volatile public dimension to the incident, for which the outcome could not have been predicted.

---

17 Charlie Brooker (January 2011) 'Disturbing Media Coverage of Raoul Moat Incident.' [YouTube]. Available from www.youtube.com/watch?v=Muz6QvLWfQQ [Accessed Nov 2019]

How infamous criminals of the likes of Moat are portrayed and influenced by the media is worth a moment of contemplation:

> Suddenly, they are shown a path where their problems won't be trivial and squalid and pointless. No: they'll be the talk of the entire country. They'll be stars.

> The way we report these cases can make that man more likely to charge out of his house to kill, or less. The psychologists say that currently we are adopting the most dangerous tactics possible. We put the killer's face everywhere. We depict him exactly as he wanted, broadcasting his videos and reading out his missives.

> We make his story famous. We present killing as its logical culmination. We soak him in glamour: look at the endless descriptions of Moat as 'having a hulking physique' and being 'a notorious hard man'.

> We present the killer as larger than life, rather than the truth: that these people are smaller than life, leading pitiful, hate-filled existences.

> —*Johann Hari* [18]

9
HUMANITY

The Raoul Moat incident showed the best and worst of human nature. On the one hand was Moat's hatred towards others: the cold-blooded execution of Christopher Brown; his cowardly shooting of Samantha Stobbart; a merciless attempt to kill PC David Rathband; and his reign of terror, unleashed on a small rural community. In contrast was the bravery, service and duty of police officers, and the strength of the community in standing together, determined that evil should not triumph. The contrasting fortunes of the many people involved not only influenced the outcome but shaped their destiny.

CHRISTOPHER BROWN

Moat, having shot and seriously injured Christopher Brown, summarily executed him at point-blank range as he lay helpless on the ground: a callous act beyond reprehension. Christopher was the man who many people, especially his family, believe was the forgotten victim. 'He was the one that was killed, but no one wants to know anything about Christopher, because there was nothing sordid or nasty,' said his mother, Sally Brown. 'He was just an everyday lad.'

Brown stumbled into the tangled web of Moat by chance. Originally from Slough in South East England, he left home in October 2009 to visit friends in Newcastle, where he stayed to pursue opportunities as a karate instructor. While knocking on doors to promote interest in his karate classes, Brown met Samantha Stobbart. Lurking in the shadows was her ex-partner Raoul Moat, who was soon to be released from prison. His prison sentence gave Samantha the opportunity to create distance and move on from her violent relationship with Moat. Her lie – telling Moat of her new relationship with a police officer, despite her knowing of his anger and resentment towards police – contributed to the fatal compromise of Christopher Brown.

On the day of Brown's death, his mother, sister and friends were enjoying a street party with neighbours outside their home in Slough. Police officers arrived to inform Sally Brown of her son's death, and joy turned to anguish, with the family in sheer disbelief.

Police family liaison officers worked closely with the family throughout, providing support at the criminal trial and at Mr Brown's inquest. One of the officers commented on how lovely, decent and dignified the Brown family were. At the request of the family, Ms Stobbart did not attend the funeral, as they blamed her for lying to Moat about Christopher being a police officer. The family felt Northumbria Police should have warned Christopher that his life was in danger.

At the funeral, white flowers and blue ribbons adorned the coffin to mark Christopher's lifelong love of Chelsea Football Club. Floral tributes in the shape of words 'Chris' and 'Daddy' dressed the hearse, and a card written by his mother read 'Christopher, love you, will always be with me. So sorry [I] was not with you like I should have, love Mum.'[19]

---

19 'Funeral of Raoul Moat victim Chris Brown is held.' BBC News Online (August 2010). Available from www.bbc.co.uk/news/uk-england-10889825 [Accessed Nov 2019]

In tribute to Christopher, and with love and respect to his mother and the Brown family, Christopher Brown will not be the unknown victim. I hope they have some degree of comfort, in the knowledge that the Northumbria Police officers involved, and the people of the North East, have the utmost sympathy and admiration for the dignity and decency shown by the family in their loss of Christopher. Gone but never forgotten.

SAMANTHA STOBBART

After the callous murder of Christopher Brown, Moat turned his revenge on his ex-partner Samantha Stobbart, blasting the shotgun through the lounge window, causing her serious abdominal injuries, which required eight hours of emergency surgery. Ms Stobbart was clearly a victim of Moat's obsessive, controlling and violent behaviour, and could not have foreseen the events that unfolded that fateful night outside her home in Birtley, Gateshead.

Samantha Stobbart met Moat at the tender age of 16 while out clubbing in Newcastle, where Moat worked on the doors. Over the next six years Moat, who was 15 years older, had a stranglehold over her life. They had a daughter together but the relationship was volatile, plagued by his jealousy and control. Moat's imprisonment gave Stobbart the opportunity to end her violent, abusive and coercive relationship.

While Stobbart has attracted much criticism for her part in pouring oil on the fire of an incendiary Moat as he awaited discharge from prison, I believe it would be wrong to lay the blame for Moat's murderous acts at the feet of Stobbart. Clearly her family background, lifestyle, education and maturity would not have prepared her – or, indeed, any 22-year-old female – for how to end a relationship with a towering, violent and unpredictable man who had control over her life. Her new partner Christopher Brown gave her a pathway to move on and create distance between herself and Moat, and yet Stobbart was looking after Moat's eight puppies while he was in prison. It was a connection that meant that Moat had a reason to call round to see her on his release. Hardly conducive to moving on, you could argue, but it maybe reflected the coercive control that Moat still held over her life.

During a phone call to Durham Prison, Samantha Stobbart told Moat the relationship was over. She taunted Moat that her new boyfriend was younger and harder, and she said he was a police officer, which she knew was untrue. She thought lying would keep him away, but it did the opposite and lit the proverbial fuse.

Following Moat's release he contacted Stobbart on 15 occasions, calling and texting her, demanding to know where she was and who she was with. At Christopher Brown's inquest Stobbart denied knowing that Moat had a gun. She thought he and Brown would have a fight, following threats from Moat that he wanted a 'straightener' with her new boyfriend. When the coroner asked what the situation might have been if and when Moat came to her house, Stobbart said, 'I did not know. I knew he would come round obviously, but I do not know because you could not predict what type of person he was.'[20]

On the evening of the incident, Stobbart and Brown returned to Birtley and called at her neighbour's house for drinks. Outside,

---

20 'I never thought that Raoul Moat would kill says Sam Stobbart.' *The Chronicle* Live (online) (December 2013). Available from https://www.chroniclelive.co.uk/news/north-east-news/ chris-brown-inquest-samantha-stobbart-6389293 [Accessed Nov 2019]

Moat was lying in wait, and the rest, as they say, is history. Christopher Brown deserved better; instead, he was treated with deceit and compromised, for which he paid the ultimate price. Who needs enemies? Ms Stobbart confessed her love for Brown, who she had just met. Whether her affection for Brown was stronger than her underlying love for Moat remains uncertain.

It is understood Ms Stobbart secured a six-figure fee from a newspaper for her story, in a deal negotiated by the now disgraced and deceased media mogul Max Clifford. If she had donated a significant part of the fee to the Brown family, or to David Rathband's charity, such a gesture would have gone some way towards demonstrating the compassion she has expressed for those victims involved.

PC DAVID RATHBAND

In the summer of 2011, I had the pleasure of meeting David at a Northumberland Pride in Volunteering event at Alnwick Castle. David appeared immaculate in his police tunic as he addressed the audience of volunteers and sponsors. I felt privileged just to be in his presence, which gave me pause for thought; how lonely life must be for David, faced with total blindness. As he spoke, the audience hung on his every word, showing a warmth, appreciation and a sense of immense pride in his resilience, in coming to terms with the pain and sadness of his loss.

David was born in Stafford in 1968. He trained as a plumber and volunteered as a special constable, serving for many years. He joined Northumbria Police in 2000, realising his ambition to be a regular police constable. Six years later, David became a motor patrols officer: his passion.

Following the devastating and life-changing impact of Moat's actions, in 2011 David established the Blue Lamp Foundation to provide support to police, fire and ambulance personnel injured in the course of duty.[21] He worked relentlessly to raise money for the charity, and his selfless dedication earned the respect of many people throughout the country, who looked on in admiration:

> I need hardly say that we have enormous admiration for the extraordinary resilience and courage you have greatly displayed. The United Kingdom owes a huge debt of gratitude to policemen like yourself who are prepared to sacrifice so much for others in the line of duty.'
>
> *—HRH The Prince of Wales*

> David was an extraordinarily brave man and after his horrific injuries he did an enormous amount for charities for other injured police officers and families who had lost police officers in the line of duty.
>
> *—Rt. Hon. David Cameron, Prime Minister 2010–16*

> In my world the word 'hero' is the way over-used. In the real world, it's the absolute minimum required for PC David Rathband.
>
> *—Alan Shearer OBE, professional footballer and broadcaster*

> In July 2010 his life changed forever when he was shot and blinded. David showed outstanding bravery in what was a terrifying situation. He was a dedicated officer who acted in the best traditions of the police service.
>
> *—Sue Sim QPM, Former Northumbria*
> *Police Chief Constable*

---

21 'Our Founder PC David Rathband'. Blue Lamp Foundation (2016). Available from www. bluelampfoundation.org/our-founder/ [Accessed Nov 2019]

On 29 February 2012, David Rathband, was found dead at his home in Blyth, Northumberland. His estranged wife, Kath Rathband, had visited David on the evening he died. After leaving the address, Kath had contacted David's force welfare officer and also sent a text message to his sister in Staffordshire, as she was concerned for his welfare. Shortly after 9:00 pm, police attended David's home, where he lived alone, to check on his wellbeing. David was found dead; he had hanged himself.

Kath told the inquest, held in Newcastle in January 2014, that, despite her concerns, she did not feel David was in imminent danger of taking his own life. She told the hearing of his affair with a 7/7 London bombing survivor, which effectively ended their marriage. Kath Rathband said that David would call her a hundred times a day asking to come home, despite having a relationship with another female. She had taken him back after previous affairs but would not do so again. 'I told him I couldn't go back [to where we were] after his behaviour to me and the kids, and he could not understand why.' Kath discovered the affair in late December 2011, before David flew to Australia to visit his brother. 'By this point, it was my opinion our marriage was over due to David's level of deceit,' she said.

Coroner Eric Armstrong ruled David Rathband took his own life.[22] In a statement read after the hearing, Kath Rathband thanked family and friends for their 'unwavering' support. 'Whilst I have lost David, he has left me with two amazing children and he would be immensely proud of them and what they

---

22 'PC David Rathband inquest.' BBC News (January 2014) Available from www.bbc.co.uk/news/uk-england-tyne-25623254 and 25652801 [Accessed Nov 2019]

achieved, as I am.' David was laid to rest at Stafford Cremato-rium.

It was a sad and tragic end to the life of a brave and proud police officer, who reached out to help others despite his cata-strophic injuries and the turmoil in his life. One would hope people do not make a judgement on David, or indeed his wife, until they have walked a mile in their shoes.

QHURAM AWAN AND KARL NESS

The involvement of Karl Ness and Qhuram Awan not only helped determine the fate of Christopher Brown, Samantha Stobbart and David Rathband, but sealed their own destiny, resulting in lengthy custodial sentences for both.

Moat's driver Qhuram Awan complained about his tough prison sentence – a minimum term of 20 years for being an accomplice to the attempted murder of a police officer. He described the sentence as double what he deserved, even though Karl Ness was given 40 years' imprisonment. In a letter appar-ently penned to a friend, Awan intimated seven or ten years would have been acceptable in the interests of justice, as he had never touched a gun let alone shot someone. While detained at Her Majesty's pleasure, Awan could make good use of his time by undertaking a law degree to better understand criminal law in relation to joint enterprise, which may cause him to reflect and consider his actions – and his victims.

Karl Ness, Moat's business partner and right-hand man, submitted an application to reduce his sentence of 40 years' minimum term. The matter was heard at an appeal hearing in London. Having been found guilty of the murder of Brown and the attempted murder of a police officer, Ness claimed his sentence was exceptional. The court judgment was summarised by Lord Judge, who stated that this was an exceptionally grave crime. 'This man [Christopher Brown] was gunned down and when the first shot did not kill him he was executed.' Lord Judge said that the injuries to PC Rathband had left him 'within a thread of death'. The Court of Appeal dismissed Ness's application.

According to his former school friends, Ness grew up as a bit of a 'jack the lad': not the sharpest tool in the box, but he knew right from wrong. In destroying the lives of others, Ness has thrown away his own – another sad and pointless aspect of this Moat saga.

PC LAWRIE WARD

Lawrie was a highly respected and approachable neighbourhood police officer, known to many in the Rothbury community. To suggest PC Ward single-handedly found Raoul Moat may not be exact in the greater scheme of things; however, it is true that Lawrie's instinctive response led to Moat's containment, for which the officer was never recognised.

If Lawrie had not responded in the way he did on receiving the information from the resident – 'He's there now' – I feel the opportunity to locate Moat at that time would have been lost. The officer could have just informed the control room of the reported sighting and left it to Communications supervision to determine the response. However, in the time it would have taken for the sighting message to be typed on the log, the incident switched to the Silver Commander to risk-assess, the caller to be recontacted for further information, and authorisation given to armed response officers to deploy, Moat would have been long gone.

Instead, PC Ward took the reins and drove at speed down the High Street to the location of the suspect male, believed armed with a gun. The officer beckoned West Yorkshire armed officers to follow him into Riverside, where Moat was located, and the seven-day manhunt was swiftly brought to an end. It is also worthy of note that Lawrie had a probationer police colleague with him at the time. The student constable normally worked out of Berwick Police Station; however, he was attached to Rothbury during the Moat incident – a memorable start to his career that I'm sure he will never forget.

Looking back at the significant role played by both officers in ending the incident, it is a great shame that while senior officers were recognised for their part in the incident – whether by promotion, increased status or acclaim – PC Lawrie Ward was overlooked. Northumbria Police were apparently waiting until after all the court proceedings, inquests and inquiries had concluded before showing appreciation to the likes of PC Ward. Unfortunately, policing moved on and the senior officers involved either retired or were promoted into other roles. If the force waits long enough, any such recognition for PC Ward will end up posthumous.

After all, PC Ward helped preserve the reputation of the force, and, to an extent, bolster the career of T/Chief Constable Sim. Most importantly, he protected his Rothbury community at a time when the media were turning and public unease was growing. Who knows where the situation would have led if Moat had not been captured at the time, through Lawrie's selfless actions.

Within 12 months Lawrie requested a transfer to Ashington, a former mining area, where policing is a different kettle of fish. (Ashington is not colloquially referred to as Ashghanistan for no reason.) His move was sudden and unexpected – maybe patrolling Rothbury was never the same. PC Ward retired in 2019; his Queen's Police Medal appears to be lost in the post.

RAOUL THOMAS MOAT

Whatever his failings, depravity or hatred, Raoul Moat was someone's son, and a father and a friend to those who knew him. Each year at 1:00 am on 10 July, as the anniversary of his death falls, his friends visit the Rothbury scene, to the chagrin of some local residents who believe the commemoration to be distasteful.

Every year I would observe the gathering at a distance, in the darkness of night, respecting their wishes to mark the passing of Raoul Thomas Moat. For an hour, cars would drive onto the grassy knoll, headlights illuminating the scene and cameras flashing as group photographs were taken. Cans of alcohol were consumed and flowers left in situ. After an hour I would politely engage with the eight or so, mainly younger, visitors. Without any bother, I would encourage the conclusion of this annual ritual, out of respect for the neighbours who overlooked the site.

Despite the vividness of the floral tributes left there, none will look better, or last longer, than the white cow parsley growing by the riverbank behind where Moat once lay, for the wildflowers that bloom in adversity are the rarest and most beautiful of them all. It seemed that, to Moat, Rothbury was a place where he was most happy and felt at ease with himself; memories, perhaps, of his time spent there in his youth. His ashes were scattered on the River Coquet, upstream from Rothbury. The river flows by the scene of his passing, the memory of which is glorified by some but held in contempt by others.

PETER BOATMAN

Who is Peter Boatman, you may ask?

When we talk about forgotten victims of the Moat incident, Peter Boatman is one who should be remembered. Mr Boatman was a retired police inspector from Northamptonshire Police, who became the director of operations at Pro-Tect Systems, the company who supplied the Tasers to Northumbria Police.

In the course of the manhunt, the Home Office inferred that police could use any weapon they saw fit, so long as its use was lawful, necessary and proportionate – the standard human rights caveat. Afterwards, Pro-Tect Systems was deemed to have breached the terms of its Home Office licence in supplying the unauthorised X12 XREP Tasers and ammunition to Northumbria Police for operational use, while it was still under testing by government scientists.

On 1 October 2010, three days after the Home Office revoked Pro-Tect System's licence to import and sell Tasers, Peter was found dead at his home in Northampton. 'He knew there was something there that would offer the officers protection and that was what his motive was. The furore over it destroyed him,' said a company director. At the inquest into his death, Northamptonshire coroner Anne Pember recorded an open verdict, with the cause of death given as carbon monoxide inhalation.[23]

Several years after his death, I attended a rural crime event in Birmingham and happened to be seated on a table with officers

---

23 'Open verdict into death of Taser supply company boss.' *The Guardian* (June 2011). Available from www.theguardian.com/uk/2011/jun/01/inquest-peter-boatman-tasers-raoul-moat

[Accessed Nov 2019]

from Northamptonshire Police. By chance, they raised Peter Boatman's name in conversation. I echo their reflection of a wonderful police inspector, sincere and genuine in every way. His death is a great loss and a travesty – influenced by the Home Office – about which one can only despair.

INSPECTOR SUE PEART

Alnwick Inspector Sue Peart exemplified the very best in leadership qualities and people skills, earning a reputation as one of the most capable, passionate and respected neighbourhood inspectors in the force. As a resident of Rothbury, she was highly regarded and trusted by her local community. From the moment Moat appeared in Rothbury, her focus was to support her officers, police staff and volunteers in engaging with the community to reassure and keep them safe.

As a former staff officer to T/Chief Constable Sue Sim, Inspector Peart was rock-solid in her support of the chief, especially when the media became overbearing and personal. She took a hit with the 'nutters' comment, made during the reading of the children's card at the police press conference. Otherwise, her visibility and strength helped retain the confidence of the community in their neighbourhood policing team. Inspector Peart's support for the welfare of her officers was exceptional.

Sue would have made an outstanding senior officer. Her dynamic, passionate and people-centred leadership style would have greatly enhanced the higher ranks, where such skills were found wanting. Unsurprisingly, the promotion rat-race was not for her, and Sue retired in 2012, together with her police inspector husband, to live in a small rural village in south-west France. On retiring, she said:

The officers who serve the public here do a fantastic job, they are committed and really care. I only hope that the community appreciate this and take time to look at policing in other areas, they will soon see just how good the police are here at Alnwick.

I would like to thank everyone who I have worked with during my time at Alnwick, especially the dedicated partners from community safety, the fire service and education. I am grateful for the support I have been given by local councillors, parish councillors and key community contacts, but my main thanks go to my police teams – they are amazing.[24]

In recognition of her distinguished police service, Sue Peart was awarded the Queen's Police Medal in June 2012. An investiture was held at Buckingham Palace, where HRH The Prince of Wales presented her medal. The award, undoubtedly well-deserved, reflected the work and commitment of Sue, and all her officers, police staff and volunteers, who were proud to have served under her leadership.

CHIEF SUPERINTENDENT MARK DENNETT

As Northumberland Area Commander, Chief Superintendent Mark Dennett held a high-profile role during the Moat incident. As Bronze Commander (reassurance), he was present in Rothbury almost daily, conducting media interviews, chairing meetings with key partners and supporting T/Chief Constable Sue Sim in engaging with the community.

Mark was a highly experienced operational commander with a firearms and critical incident background. He had an ear to

---

24 'Inspector calls it a day.' *Northumberland Gazette* (January 2012) Available at www. northumberlandgazette.co.uk

the ground, sensing officer frustrations and praising the work of the local neighbourhood police team, which he championed in submissions to the Home Office.

Chief Superintendent Dennett retired in 2012, when he became Deputy Police and Crime Commissioner for Northumbria. He stood down from the role in 2014, to follow his passion for motorcycle touring.

CHIEF SUPERINTENDENT NEIL ADAMSON

As Northumbria Police Head of Crime, Chief Superintendent Neil Adamson became the public face of the police enquiry to bring Moat and his accomplices to justice. Daily press briefings were fronted by Chief Supt. Adamson, accompanied by T/Chief Constable Sue Sim. As an experienced career detective, Neil was thoughtful and methodical throughout, resulting in the successful convictions of, and substantial prison sentences for, Karl Ness and Qhuram Awan.

In the years following the Moat incident, Chief Supt. Adamson's working relationship with Chief Constable Sim could be best described as functional and respectful – Christmas cards were unlikely to have been exchanged. Subsequent representations made by a number of senior police officers in respect of Chief Constable Sim proved to be a turning point in her career. Neil Adamson retired in 2018 to enjoy the fruits of his labour.

SUPERINTENDENT JO FARRELL

As Silver Commander on duty when Moat shot PC Rathband, and also in charge when he took his own life, the Moat incident was a baptism of fire for Superintendent Farrell. In career terms, she came of age. Her career began in Cambridgeshire Constabulary, then in 2002 she transferred to Northumbria Police as chief inspector. Having been identified as chief officer material, she was supported by the force in a portfolio of roles on her journey to the higher echelons of power.

I recall, a few years before Moat, attending a Silver Command critical incident management training course as communications sergeant, and Chief Inspector Jo Farrell was part of our group. During training scenarios I found her critical incident knowledge and experience rather limited; however, her willingness to listen was clearly apparent, and her razor-sharp grasp of the issues and pleasant demeanour gave the impression she was going places.

Following the Moat incident, the level of scrutiny of Superintendent Farrell's leadership, decision-making and operational competence was unprecedented. IPCC enquiries, inquests and civil court cases all served to validate her professional judgement and recognise her capabilities in the Silver Commander role performed.

Supt. Farrell was rapidly promoted to Assistant Chief Constable, and then in 2016 she transferred to the post of Deputy Chief Constable in the neighbouring Durham Constabulary force. In 2019, Jo Farrell was promoted to Chief Constable of Durham Constabulary, a well-deserved, fitting appointment.

ASSISTANT CHIEF CONSTABLE STEVE ASHMAN

As a former Territorial Support Group inspector in the Metropolitan Police, Assistant Chief Constable Steve Ashman was a highly capable 'street cop', who significantly enhanced the leadership and operational experience of the Chief Officer team. His decisive leadership as Gold Commander, especially in sanctioning the use of XREP Tasers as a last resort to save life, showed his strength of character. Immediately after the Moat incident, Mr Ashman toured the force to thank officers and provide an overview of the incident from a chief officer perspective, which was highly impressive.

In 2015, Steve Ashman was appointed Chief Constable of Northumbria Police, in the middle of a decade of the most savage government cuts to police and the criminal justice system. Police officer posts were cut nationally by over 20,000 officers, police staff posts reduced by 23,000 and hundreds of police stations were closed. The Right Honourable Theresa May was to policing what Doctor Beeching was to the railways in the 1960s.

Mr Ashman, and his predecessor Mrs Sim, realised Northumbria Police, with unprecedented budget cuts and the loss of more than a thousand police officers, would have to revolutionise how the force conducted police business, to face up to future threats of terrorism, sexual exploitation and cybercrime. Chief Constable Ashman brought a new freshness across the force. He empowered his commanders to manage their multi-million-pound budgets as they saw fit, and he understood the choppy waters ahead, the challenges of keeping morale high and the need for everyone to ride the waves in uncertain times. Mr Ashman implemented the 'Proud' agenda. The Proud (to Serve) vision and values were robustly instilled in every officer and across all levels of leadership, transforming the culture within Northumbria Police.

Steve Ashman would have made an excellent commissioner of the Metropolitan Police when the vacancy arose in 2017, although the political nature of such appointments may have restricted his suitability for the role, if indeed he had any such thoughts of moving from his native North East back to the capital, where his police career first began. Chief Constable Ashman retired in 2017, leaving a legacy of one of the more dynamic, reforming and operational-savvy chief constables in the history of the force.

T/CHIEF CONSTABLE SUE SIM

Sue Sim joined Merseyside Police as a graduate entrant in 1985 and transferred to Northumbria Police as Assistant Chief Constable in 2004. Mrs Sim rose to the rank of Temporary Chief Constable and oversaw one of the biggest manhunts in UK history.

As the public face of Northumbria Police, T/Chief Constable Sim showed a steely determination to overcome the challenges of the Moat incident and the growing concerns over the force's ability to manage it. Despite personal attacks from sections of the media, Mrs Sim remained steadfast in her resolve to keep the people of Rothbury safe and bring Moat to justice. Her presence on the streets of Rothbury, and personable style in engaging with members of the local community, earned her trust and respect. This approach contrasted sharply with many senior officers in such situations, who would often present as aloof and distant to the communities they served.

In an outlandish way, one could draw comparisons between Mrs Sim and Prime Minister Margaret Thatcher. Mrs Sim and Mrs Thatcher both needed positive outcomes to secure their careers; failure would result in a loss of credibility and careers down the pan. As it turned out, both were fortuitous in their outcomes. A British victory in the Falklands War in 1982 led Mrs Thatcher to a second term in office, and the positive outcome of the Moat incident led to Mrs Sim's permanent appointment as Chief Constable of Northumbria Police; the first female chief constable to lead a metropolitan police force in UK history. The Rothbury community were extremely grateful for her unwavering loyalty; mutual trust and admiration for Mrs Sim holds firm to this day.

Despite having to oversee the deepest budget cuts of any force in the country, resulting in the loss of hundreds of police officer posts, Chief Constable Sim was determined, as far as possible, to preserve neighbourhood policing as the cornerstone of Northumbria Police. Rothbury had not merely influenced her thinking but affirmed her belief in neighbourhood policing. Most other police forces targeted neighbourhood officer reductions to address the severe financial constraints, which will be much to their detriment in the longer term.

Chief Constable Sim took great strides in supporting female officers to achieve higher positions in leadership, evident in the wider use of temporary promotions in senior officer ranks, to support their progression. Her commitment to front-line operational officers was strong. On occasions when those officers expressed concerns, Mrs Sim would often confront senior managers, holding their feet to the fire. She had a fierce reputation for breaking down organisation barriers to get things done, which was not always appreciated by senior colleagues. Mrs Sim's leadership style has been described as dictatorial and overly intrusive – making policy on the hoof and shouting at senior officers. Those who upset or challenged her risked being bounced to other roles or departments, or back to Area Command.

Bearing similarities to Mrs Thatcher's downfall, which was instigated by disgruntled cabinet colleagues in 2015, Chief Constable Sim was subject to complaints by senior officers, alleging bullying. A misconduct investigation concluded that the chief constable had no case to answer on breaching police standards. However, apologies were sought from Mrs Sim in respect of two officers, and there was a requirement for her to undertake management training if she remained in the force. Mrs Sim retired that same year, after completing 30 years' service.

Following retirement, Mrs Sim hit back with allegations of sexism and a money-grabbing boys club amongst senior officers. Her claims were investigated by the new Northumbria Police Chief Constable, Steve Ashman, with independent police misconduct oversight. Her claims were not supported; furthermore, the four staff associations representing Northumbria Police jointly stated they did not recognise the picture she painted.

Instead of retiring gracefully, a rather scorned Mrs Sim hit the media headlines, instigated much by her own volition, which at times became a little unedifying. Her legacy, while somewhat tainted in her final moments, will surely reflect the success of her leadership in the Raoul Moat incident: restructuring the force to manage austere budget cuts, her passion for neighbourhood policing, and compassion to do the very best for her communities. Chief Constable Sim should be rightly proud of her achievements in upholding the reputation of Northumbria Police as one of the best-performing forces in the country.

ELIZABETH CLIFTON

Rothbury resident Elizabeth Clifton would stand for none of this Raoul Moat threat to her community baloney. As Elizabeth pointed out when stopped at an armed police checkpoint, she had served in communications during the war and was not in the slightest scared of 'that bugger'.

As a valued Police Support Volunteer at over 90 years of age, Elizabeth remained active in the Rothbury community. She proofread the *Over the Bridges* church and community magazine and, among many other things, she supported the local parish church, where she donated a significant sum to renovate the church organ.

Sadly, Elizabeth died in February 2017, aged 92 years. She was a source of so much love and goodwill, and the world is most definitely a better place for having been graced with her presence. Elizabeth will be remembered as a kind, generous, intelligent, strong-willed and free-thinking woman – a strong role model whose entire life was dedicated to the service of her country and her community.

Elizabeth represented the very best in humanity, reflecting how the police and community came together to support each other in times of need – the true legacy of the Moat incident.

10
COLD WIND
OF CHANGE

With a sense of normality having returned to the village, and thoughts of Moat slowly diminishing, Rothbury's character had lost some of its idyllic charm and innocence. The village, nonetheless, still retained a vibrancy, warmth and neighbourly feel following its rise to prominence. Rothbury was now firmly on the map on the back of a free national 'marketing campaign'. Tourists flocked in their droves to its ancient landmarks, hills and country estates. Due to the added visitor interest in Moat, a rather unconventional sightseeing attraction emerged: the scene of Moat's last stand.

From a Northumbria Police perspective, the neighbourhood policing of Moat was acknowledged as highly successful. The Home Office recognised the incident as an example of best practice, from which local officers took much pride. Above all, maintaining the trust, confidence and consent of the local community should be the cornerstone of any civilised state and police organisation.

POLICING IN AUSTERITY

Following the Moat incident in 2010, for the next decade a cold wind of change – austerity – blew across policing and other public services, severely affecting the communities they served. Neighbourhood police teams in every town and village were suddenly under threat, with officers deemed dispensable under cost-cutting measures. Police forces retreated towards a more reactive model of policing, which would have serious ramifications for community policing throughout the country.

The Conservative government, under Home Secretary Theresa May, made a political decision to target the police with the most severe central government funding cuts in history, despite grave warnings from bodies representing the police. Mrs May claimed reductions in police budgets did not lead to increases in crime, which, to many, appeared to defy common sense. If a government withdraws investment in the police and communities, crime is only going to go one way; the resultant pain and suffering would take at least a generation to recover from. In 2015, Mrs May addressed the annual conference of the Police Federation, an organisation that represents rank and file officers in England and Wales:

> Over the past five years we've had to make some tough and difficult decisions. We have reformed your pay and pensions, reduced police spending and yes, there are fewer officers overall. But despite the predictions of the federation and despite the predictions of the politicians, who wanted to sell you a false dream of ever more spending, crime is down by more than a quarter since 2010, according to the Independent Crime Survey for England and Wales. This weekend, the federation warned that spending reductions mean that we'll be 'forced to adopt a paramilitary style of policing in Britain.' Today, you said that neighbourhood police officers are an endangered species. I have to tell you, that this kind of scaremongering does nobody any good. It

doesn't serve you, it doesn't serve the officers you represent and it doesn't serve the public.[25]

Over the tenure of her leadership, from 2010 to 2019, over 20,000 police officer posts were lost, thousands of police staff were made redundant and hundreds of police stations were closed. Court buildings were abandoned, including in Alnwick, with over half of the magistrates courts in England and Wales closed, and a disastrous probation service privatisation led to renationalisation. The state of the prison service was in crisis. Local authorities were cut to the bone, with non-essential community services and partnerships downsized or axed due to financial constraints.

Despite warnings that cuts have consequences, Mrs May's assertion that reductions in police budgets did not correlate to increases in crime was short lived. As the cuts took effect, all areas of the country suffered significant increases in crime. An epidemic of knife crime and violent crime led to stabbings and murders spiralling. Cybercrime became unmanageable and severe terrorism threats were at the highest level. Community confidence in policing and public services was at rock bottom.

WHAT DID THIS MEAN FOR ROTHBURY?

The harshest cuts were felt across the vast rural areas of the country, with Northumberland in particular feeling the blunt instrument of austerity. In Rothbury, neighbourhood officers were reduced in numbers, down from four to three constables,

---

25 Speech given by Home Secretary Theresa May at the Police Federation annual conference, May 2015. Available from www.gov.uk/government/speeches/home-secretarys-police-federation-2015-speech. [Accessed Nov 2019]

and the sergeant's post was abolished, to be covered by the Alnwick neighbourhood sergeant. Officers were tasked to patrol a larger geographical area, responding primarily to incidents, with neighbourhood policing becoming rather superficial. Following internal force boundary changes, Alnwick sector even acquired a local prison on the patch – HMP Northumberland, with over 1,300 inmates. A Rothbury officer queried whether his role had changed to prison liaison officer, having spent a significant amount of his duty time responding to and dealing with incidents at the prison.

Across the Alnwick sector, the number of police–community support officers decreased, and Alnwick CID, motor patrols and dog section officers were reduced and displaced to work from centralised hubs in distant towns. In effect, this rendered coverage of rural areas virtually non-existent. Area Support Groups (units of specialist public order and search officers) were disbanded and Alnwick 24/7 response sergeants were transferred to other policing sectors, with the sergeants at Berwick, some 40 miles away, acquiring responsibility to supervise Alnwick, a decision that was reversed several years later.

Police custody suites were closed, and rural police officers regularly had to transport prisoners over 30 miles to custody suites in North Tyneside and Newcastle – the equivalent of arresting a person in Manchester and having to transport the prisoner to Liverpool. Critical low levels of police resourcing became the norm due to minimum staffing and officer abstractions. Vast swathes of rural Northumberland were often devoid of officers, especially at night time. Well-established and highly effective police–community and multi-agency partnerships were obliterated, with public trust and confidence in the police waning.

In 2019, the Rothbury Police Office was closed. Local officers were relocated to a building shared with Northumberland National Park Authority, just off Rothbury High Street.[26] The move annoyed some residents living nearby, who were unable to park their cars due to police vehicles left almost permanently in the street, with no police officers in sight. The press release and accompanying photograph trumpeted the move to the new police room, and the force wheeled out a superintendent, inspector and neighbourhood sergeant, all stationed elsewhere, for the photo opportunity. The community were informed that the move would see no change in how the area was policed and the neighbourhood police team would continue to patrol and operate in the community.

Comments from the Northumbria Police and Crime Commissioner and the Northumberland Police Commander were carefully crafted to reassure the community. The area commander said:

> I want to make it clear to the public that this change does not affect our commitment and dedication to the communities we serve. Neighbourhood policing is a top priority for us and we will continue to do everything we can to deliver an outstanding service.

Sadly, within a year officers no longer worked directly from the Rothbury police room. Instead, they started and finished their duties at Alnwick Police Station, 12 miles away. Apparently, only one neighbourhood officer and a PCSO (when they are

---

26 'Northumbria Police set to move to new base secured for officers in Rothbury.' Northumbria Police (May 2019). Available from https://beta.northumbria.police.uk/latest-news/2019/may/northumbria-police-set-to-move-to-new-base-secured-for-officers-in-rothbury/ [Accessed 2019]

on duty) travel across to patrol the town of Rothbury and rural Coquetdale. Alnwick response officers will attend emergencies, or incidents that cannot be dealt by other means, otherwise the community is left to police itself. Even local police volunteers are no more, due to lack of support and encouragement. Rothbury residents living in houses adjacent to the dormant police post report the occasional visit by an officer. On a more positive note, they are now able to park their cars on the street.

Empty words from commanders and commissioners serve no purpose in maintaining the trust and confidence of the community. The Rothbury neighbourhood policing footprint has been reduced to a shadow of its former self, and community concerns have been growing, not only in Rothbury, but across the rural landscape of North Northumberland, that crime has become progressively worse and police are not taking rural crime seriously or putting adequate resources into Northumberland. Without sounding too repetitive, if a police force withdraws investment in policing and communities, crime is only going to go one way.

Several centuries ago, the Border Reivers were given free range along the Anglo-Scottish border, to roam and pillage remote baron lands and isolated Northumberland village settlements, undefended by anyone in authority. Parallels can be drawn between the Border Reivers of yesterday and the travelling rural criminals of today.

A DIMINISHING FORCE

Policing in many parts of the UK was ravaged by austerity, officer reductions, restructuring and fragmentation. Where does the blame lie for this systematic destruction of a police institution, once the envy of the world? Unquestionably, at the door of the Home Office and 10 Downing Street, where the incumbent Theresa May presided over a slash-and-burn approach. The government washed their hands of any long-term policing vision; instead, they introduced local police and crime commissioners, so ministers responsible for the debacle could publicly shift the blame to others. Chickens have indeed come home to roost, with significant rises in recorded crime, just as the Police Federation warned – pathetically dismissed by May as scaremongering.

Northumbria Police were faced with the biggest cuts of any police force in the country. Chief officers had difficult decisions to make, which inevitably impacted on people's lives. They had little choice but to restructure the way the organisation conducted its police business to make the most of scarce resources. The force prioritised the fight against terrorism, serious and organised crime, safeguarding vulnerable people and tackling cybercrime. Policing as we knew it would have to change, and communities would take a hit. The six Area Commands were merged into three, with Northumberland and North Tyneside absorbed into the new Northern Area Command, headed by a chief superintendent based in Wallsend, North Tyneside.

With Northern Area Command now the size of Luxembourg, it was apparent that police officers were being sucked towards the newly formed, more urban, centralised hubs, which caused a greater disconnect from distant rural Northumberland communities. Understandably, there is more bang for your buck in locating police resources in the largest urban population centres to tackle serious criminality, volume crime and anti-social behaviour. Recorded crime increased across the Area Command, which adversely affected public trust and confidence in local policing, especially in remote Northumberland.

The job of managing such large Area Commands (bigger than some UK police forces) was maybe too big for some senior commanders. Police forces still have senior officers who started life pounding the beat leading departments and Area Commands but, while they are well-meaning, they probably know very little about running efficient organisations with vast resources in a rapidly changing policing environment. Senior police management gave an impression of having a limited understanding of rural communities, and less prominence was given to them, with crime perceived as low and far removed from everyday Area Command business.

Policing was slowly but surely gravitating towards a paramilitary-style response force. Officers wore unsightly mix-and-match black uniforms with multi-gadget utility belts. Many senior officers declined to wear the replacement combat police uniform, as if it were beneath their status. If police officers are no longer seen to be visibly engaging with the public then communities are less inclined to see themselves as part of the police, and public support in future incidents such as Moat may not be as forthcoming. As a case in point, there have been recent decisions by police forces, including Northumbria Police, for officers not to attend Remembrance events in towns and villages, blaming austerity and lack of resources (during a quiet November period of low police demand). These reasons don't really wash, and such officer absence gives the community the impression that the police are disinterested and detached.

All things said, chief officers, commissioners, police officers and staff of Northumbria Police were unwavering in their determination to keep the wheels of policing going to protect communities as far as possible and they strove to achieve the very best with so little. The government's decision to devolve responsibility for elements of police funding, from central government to local council taxpayers, may work in prosperous Surrey but not in the more deprived force areas such as Northumbria Police, where the potential to generate additional revenue has its limitations. The financial challenges for forces were so great that some elements of policing had to give.

AN ENDANGERED SPECIES

Several chief constables held strong views that neighbourhood officers were dispensable. When he faced losing 40% of his officers, former Chief Constable of Merseyside Police Sir Jon Murphy warned that savage cuts to policing will result in 'human tragedy'. He has been a beat officer during the Toxteth riots in Liverpool in 1981, and in 2015 he gave an interview to the *Liverpool Echo*. Mr Murphy said that policing had come a long way since then, but the cuts risked destroying that good work:

> The notion of neighbourhood policing, having a relationship with the community, was not present and we paid the price for it. I think that all of the gains that we have made over the last 30 years in terms of building relationships with communities will be under threat [...]

> Whether the public like it or not, whether the media like it or not, whether politicians like it or not, neighbourhood policing is the discretionary part of our business [...] Put it this way, if we don't monitor a sex offender properly and we lose them it could result in something catastrophic for a young person. For the sake of having two officers walking

the beat in high-visibility coats, I would be reducing our ability to have officers in a more effective position where they can manage the threat, harm and risk posed to our communities [...]

I think most of the public would say I need the police to do the job that is required when I need them to do it. In times such as we're in, that's more important than being seen and visible [...] Different chiefs will make different decisions according to the problems present in their particular force. For me the most important thing is keeping the public safe.[27]

Sir Jon Murphy highlighted that police-recorded crime was rising and cybercrimes were unrecorded. From 2015, crimes involving violence, guns, knives, sex offences and murders began to significantly increase, contrary to Mrs May's assertions at the Police Federation conference. Mr Murphy, as Chief Police Officer lead for crime, also addressed the Superintendents Association conference in 2013, where he was quoted by the Police Oracle website, in respect to neighbourhood policing:

'I don't see firefighters, paramedics or nurses walking the streets in case somebody becomes ill,' Mr Murphy reportedly said, and there was a 'political and public obsession' with police visibility 'irrespective of actual neighbourhood demand. Which is more important – deploying resources in big hats or high-visibility jackets to make the public feel safe or focusing on what is less visible to the public but actually does protect them from serious harms such as child sex abuse, cybercrime or serious organised crime?'

---

27 'Merseyside's chief constable Sir Jon Murphy predicts "human tragedy" as he faces losing 40% of his officers.' *The Liverpool Echo* online (Nov 2015). Available from www.liverpoolecho.co.uk/news/liverpool-news/merseysides-chief-constable-sir-jon-10437202 [Accessed Nov 2019]

Steady on, Sir Jon – remember Toxteth!

We might have hoped that Peter Singleton, former chairman of the Merseyside Police Federation, would put his big hat on and stand up for his hard-working neighbourhood colleagues, policing on the front line in his Merseyside communities. He was quoted in the *Independent, saying*:

> Chief officers in Merseyside now know that if there are youths on the street playing football or causing disturbance, nobody dies. If we get the firearms problem wrong, people will die – it's as simple as that.
>
> Our chief officers have tried to preserve the front line, but they aren't able to anymore.[28]

Wow! Not much love for neighbourhood wooden tops, walking around estates in Merseyside. For some unknown reason, chiefs don't correlate such stereotypical views on the visibility of neighbourhood officers with firearms officers deployed in pairs, riding around in swanky BMW cars, tooled up with an array of weapons, faces beaming like Cheshire cats, sporting shades, and baseball caps, in case a firearms incident was to happen.

To suggest neighbourhood police officers just walk the streets 'in case somebody becomes ill' (read: commits a crime) is equivalent to the ignorance of my suggesting firearms officers do nothing other than the occasional firearms deployment. Both firearms and neighbourhood officers are tasked to keep the public safe; respectively, they conduct targeted interventions to

---

28 'No future for bobbies on the beat, claims senior police officer.' *The Independent* online (September 2013). Available from www.independent.co.uk/news/uk/crime/no-future-for-bobbies-on-the-beat-claims-senior-police-officer-8812956.html [Accessed Nov 2019]

deter, disrupt and divert crime linked to firearms, and crime and disorder impacting on communities, including serious crime.

The views of some chief officers (not our very own Mrs Sim, I hasten to add), were likely due to their lack of understanding of the actual role performed by our neighbourhood officers, which could be summarised as:

- develop police–community relationships and gather community intelligence
- initiate early interventions with local partner to prevent and target crime and disorder
- tackle anti-social behaviour and promote diversionary initiatives to address youth disorder
- engage with the vulnerable, hard-to-reach and potentially problematic
- implement safeguarding plans for victims of domestic violence abuse and repeat-crime victims
- support multi-agency working to protect vulnerable people at risk of harm
- supervise licensed premises, support tenancy enforcement and criminal behaviour orders
- respond to incidents including emergency response, beat crimes and disorder
- show a visible presence in neighbourhoods (if time), by wearing a big hat and high-visibility coat
- work in the heart of communities to keep people safe and build trust and confidence in policing.

In essence, the preceding points are about ensuring the community is part of the police and the police remain part of the community – because only by working together will the absence of crime be achieved. It is as simple as that.

Effective neighbourhood policing reduces crime, disorder, vulnerability, incident demand, domestic violence, drugs, stabbings, murders, terrorism … the list goes on. It is preferable to having to respond to such incidents that then result in costly CID investigations, firearms operations, specialist searches, forensic examinations, custody procedures, criminal submissions, courts and the rest. Not to mention the detrimental effect on communities and victims in trying to shut the stable door after the horse had bolted.

One of Sir Robert Peel's Principles of Law Enforcement (see Appendix) states:

> The test of police efficiency is the absence of crime and disorder, not the visible evidence of police action in dealing with it.

Let's not forget that the investment in neighbourhood policing in Rothbury and most other communities across the country led to lower crime and safer environments, unlike the lack of neighbourhood involvement in the eighties. Remember Toxteth, Broadwater Farm, Moss Side, and the many towns and cities where crime spiralled out of control and policing by consent broke down, giving way to serious violence and disorder. Buildings burned and, sadly, lives were lost. Rural villages are not immune. The broken window effect, in the absence of police, leads to a gradual contagion of crime and disorder in neighbourhoods, and is much harder to resolve once criminality takes hold.

The author JB Priestley, in the play *An Inspector Calls*, alludes to the consequences for any government that ignores the plight of communities and the people who suffer the consequences:

We don't live alone. We are members of one body. We are responsible for each other. And I tell you that the time will soon come when if men will not learn that lesson, then they will be taught it in fire and blood and anguish.[29]

Governments and chief constables would do well to take heed of those wise words; all people, all communities and neighbourhood policing, matter.

11
REFLECTION
AND PRIDE

In today's uncertain climate, the Moat incident seems so long ago, although it is wise to never drop your guard. Events such as manhunts, pandemics or riots come from nowhere, and a gunman terrorising a community will happen again, in some unsuspecting village, town or city in the UK. If a repeat incident were to take place in Northumbria, how would the force respond? Have Northumbria Police learned the lessons of the Moat incident?

LESSONS LEARNED

Changes to Communications department procedures would result in urgent radio broadcasts and warnings immediately circulated to patrol officers where an armed threat to police officers has been identified. A pre-planned response would be activated, to negate the risk to unarmed officers, which may lessen the likelihood of another victim like PC Rathband. The substantial investment by the force in firearms resources and capabilities to tackle terrorism will strengthen any initial armed police response.

The jury is still out on whether communications, command and control, information handing and the silo-hierarchical mentality has improved. Specialised police search resources were disbanded; hopefully, there will be enough search-trained officers still available to regroup and provide some level of capability. Search strategies involving open countryside should be better informed in the aftermath of the Moat incident, even though the promised force debrief for Northumberland National Park Authority – to share their learning, having worked closely with the search teams – never materialised. Police officer feedback submissions, especially in relation to those unarmed officers placed in danger, appeared to have vanished into thin air. The increased availability of firearms resources and the wider roll-out of Tasers to neighbourhood and response officers is welcome. How to protect unarmed officers when a direct firearms threat is made remains unanswered.

In London, in March 2017, unarmed Police Constable Keith Palmer was stabbed to death while on duty at the gates of the Houses of Parliament, despite the UK terrorism threat level having been assessed as severe (i.e. an attack is highly likely). At the time, armed police officers were nowhere to be seen, and the knife-wielding terrorist suspect was shot dead by a plain-clothes ministerial protection officer who, by chance, was in the immediate vicinity at the time. Ironically, a police commissioner was also close by but remained locked inside his car for his own personal safety. Police officers are repeatedly told they are not averse to risk in performing their duties. Chief officers should not be seen as having an exemption from such risks, responsibilities or accountability.

In any given police situation, failings in leadership, in not affording reasonable protection to officers commensurate to the threat known or believed at the time, should result in severe sanction. Criminal proceedings against police forces should be considered where the offence of corporate manslaughter is evident. Only then will the safety of officers be given greater prominence, and the decision to issue light firearms for their protection, whether in Westminster, Rothbury or elsewhere, be more likely.

With respect to Moat, the likelihood of a future similar incident happening in a well-policed and resilient Northumberland neighbourhood is remote. Policing across the force has contracted, local partnership working has declined and community engagement has weakened. Rural residents, other than in emergencies, experience delayed incident response, telephone resolution or infrequent officer patrols, which provide negligible reassurance and visibility.

Occasionally, Northumbria Police will create the impression of fighting crime in rural areas through positive media releases. A senior officer will don an operational police uniform and have a photograph taken on a quad bike. The police and crime commissioner will promote herself wearing wellies while visiting a farm, to highlight police tackling rural crime. A symbolic Rothbury Police Office will present as a bastion of the community, but it stands empty, more or less permanently closed, absent of police, and the community is unable to visit. In effect, the force promotes publicity opportunities with the aim of positively influencing the public's perception of rural policing without much operational substance behind the initiatives. The public will get wind of this common practice someday.

REFLECTION

Austerity has clearly affected rural Northumberland. Many communities feel left behind with regard to broadband, employment, policing, affordable housing, public transport and inflated fuel costs. One would hope the government decision to reverse the cuts in officer numbers will serve to re-establish visible neighbourhood policing. Perhaps residents will look back at the Moat era with an air of nostalgia, in terms of policing, community spirit and feeling protected. In an interview with the *Northumberland Gazette*, former Alnwick Police inspector and Rothbury resident Sue Peart reflected on the events of July 2010:

> There was a massive amount of pressure put on me and my team during this [incident], but as I said to my boss; myself and the team are up to whatever they want to throw at us. We had a number of police officers who worked locally and lived in the village. That made it even more difficult for the local team as they had loved ones here, children here and their homes were here. So, as well as working long hours, which we were happy to do, we were living and breathing it at work and at home knowing that this case was going on in your village. There was added risk and added stress for a lot of officers but not one shirked from that. It was an example of the strength of the community working with the police.
>
> Our best intelligence suggested Moat was in or around the village and he was targeting police officers. Despite these threats, one of the neighbourhood policing team on a rest day said, 'I am coming in, it is my village.' Another was on holiday in the south of the country. He drove up and was in work for 8:00 am the next morning. He said there are four police officers who police the area and one of them isn't there. That's the kind of community we are. And that is why I am so proud of the officers. In spite of being in what I would consider to be very real danger, they still came in from days off, put themselves on duty and at risk, and went home to the same thing.
>
> Since coming here I have been committed to engaging with

the public because I think that is the most effective way of policing the rural areas. The work I have done in setting up things like Farm Watch with the excellent work of PC Katrina Cassidy, really came into play. During the investigation it was a way of getting information out to people on farms. We were contacting them twice a day as they were bound to feel more vulnerable being isolated. Our community messaging service, which was set up, was also used. A huge number of the community received email updates about the situation and we used the emergency text service for the first time when the village went into lockdown.

Not only was the policing team dealing with a huge incident, they were also dealing with a huge amount of armed officers using their small station. It was interesting having our little police station full of hundreds of armed officers. Thankfully, the gallery upstairs opened up to help us accommodate them all. At one point the drains started to overflow because the toilet was being used so much, and we only had one kettle for them all to make cups of tea, but the community pitched in.

The Jubilee Hall committee was absolutely tremendous. They provided accommodation for police officers on the breaks, and use of the kitchen and other facilities. Members of the public offered them cups of tea when they were out. We had officers from 18 forces here. I made a point of individually welcoming them and thanking them for coming to help us support and protect the village through this unprecedented incident; their response was 'It's a pleasure'. They said the community were wonderful and they liked the place.

I think had it not been for the work of my neighbourhood team over two-and-a-half years, trying to gain trust and confidence with the public, it wouldn't be like that. The police are part of this community. We held a reassurance forum with local business leaders, parish councillors and other key members of the community before holding the community forum during the week when Moat was in Rothbury. I said to them 'trust me' and I will do everything I can to protect my community. They did trust me and we all came through it.[30]

The safety of Rothbury schoolchildren was a great concern for many parents following the threat from Moat to harm innocent members of the community. Armed police officers were permanently posted to Dr Thomlinson C of E Middle School to protect the children and staff and reassure parents. Headteacher Heather Cape looked back at the challenges and anxious moments for all concerned:

All week we felt the police considered the school as a high priority and we were continually thought of in relation to the current situation and the safety of the children. The police (both armed and uniform officers) were fantastic: they were friendly and reassuring. As a result of their professionalism you now have many budding police officers desperate to join the ranks from our school.

The presence of the police throughout the day and at the beginning and ending of the school day was a great reassurance and appreciated by both staff and parents. If I am honest, there were times throughout the week when I did wonder whether we were doing the right thing in opening the school, as we felt vulnerable and at times quite frightened about the 'what ifs'. Without a constant police presence I am not sure whether I would have actually been prepared to pull 200 children into school and kept it open.

---

30 'Community champions.' *Northumberland Gazette* (July 2010). Available from www. northumberlandgazette.co.uk

Communication throughout the week with the school was challenging. At times our phone lines were jammed by worried parents preventing people like yourself [police] and also County Hall phoning. This was exacerbated by mobile networks also going down throughout the day. A liaison officer posted at the school, particularly on the Tuesday, would have greatly helped this problem (especially if this was one of the community officers we know from our local police).

Things also became very confused when, at the end of Tuesday, my instructions from Gold Command, and their links with the resilience team at County Hall, to keep the children in lockdown was contrasting to the sergeant advice at the school, saying road blocks had been told to let the buses through and it was safe for children to go.

Perhaps things were changing so quickly on the ground before Gold Command knew the changes to the situation? At times I was not sure which instructions were the ones we should be following. This was made worse by the fact the press (Sky News and BBC News) announced on the TV that parents should go to collect their children before we were given the go-ahead on the ground for this to happen.

Similar problems were encountered on the Wednesday morning, when the early news announced police had stated schools would be open as normal. At this point I had not conversed with anyone from the police, council or other headteachers to make this decision. Being consulted on whether the school should open, by whoever made the decision and informed the press would have been appreciated.

I cannot begin to imagine what managing such a huge operation would have been like, and please take the two points made above not as a criticism but purely as a 'Would have been better if …'.

I am totally supportive of the police and how they conducted the operation. At no point through the week was the community upset by the presence of the police and this was down to their professional manner and the way they openly communicated with all, from the open public meetings to the community leaders' meetings.

This has continued to be the case since last Friday. Rothbury Station (in particular PC Kilburn) have readily agreed to keep a close eye on events such as the school disco, school events at the Rothbury Music Festival and pupil traffic surveys as one or two parents still feel anxious due to the higher amounts of 'unwanted' visitors around the town.

My own personal and sincere thanks to you personally for your support throughout the week. I think the police did a fantastic job and I know why Northumbria Police is seen as one of the most professional forces in the country.[31]

PRIDE

In the aftermath of the Moat incident, a semblance of normal village life returned. The community quietly went about their daily routines with a sense of purpose, wellbeing and ordinariness. In the weeks that followed, as summer drew to a close, visitor numbers dwindled and the last remnants of people connected with Moat left the village (and the police station). At last, I had a moment to draw breath. The tumultuous events of July only really started to sink in when routine became reality once more.

Alone in the back room of Rothbury Police Office, I decided to review the progress of the 2010 summer policing plan, which

---

31 Heather Cape (2010), personal correspondence to author, with permission.

had been gathering dust. The Moat incident, in many respects, had rendered the document irrelevant. I decided to cut my losses and file the plan until the following year. With an undisturbed, peaceful moment to myself I was able to collect my thoughts and, for a moment, I asked myself – did this incident really happen, or was it all just a dream? Was I hallucinating, imagining an armed gunman on the run, hundreds of armed police in the village, officers taking refuge in this small police office and the world's media in Rothbury broadcasting an armed stand-off that led to the death of the suspect? Did that all really take place in this quaint old Northumberland village?

If, during the Moat incident, a couple of local residents had miraculously been rowing across the Atlantic, trekking across the North Pole, or journeying through the Amazon rainforest, and on their return home visited Rothbury Police Office where I explained recent events to them, they would probably have thought I was barking mad.

It was a dynamic event for sure, with many mixed emotions – fear, anger, sadness, anticipation and relief. Moat's irrational threat to harm a member of the public for each lie told by the media had to be taken face value, with the absolute need to protect residents. But, in a village where he took great comfort, would he have *actually* harmed a Rothbury resident he had no personal grievance against? That remains uncertain. The media hype clearly took on a momentum of its own, at a scale of unbelievable disproportion.

As I reflected on a momentous summer, I would be lying if I said I didn't feel a touch of emotion and pride – in my colleagues, in our wonderful community and in Northumbria Police in coming through the ultimate challenge any police force, neighbourhood policing team or village could ever face. This was a community and police organisation where we genuinely cared about each other. There is an enormous amount of pride and spirit in Rothbury and beyond: everyone knows each other; we all value and respect one another; and we always come together in times of need. It's been a privilege to have served and been part of the community.

As I sat reminiscing, rationalising my thoughts – or rather, daydreaming again – I opened the rear exit door of the police station to allow some much-needed fresh air to circulate on yet another beautiful sunny day. I recall thinking, 'Despite all that's gone on, isn't life good.' The peaceful ambience was short lived and the tranquillity abruptly shattered as the station buzzer sounded, indicating someone at the front counter. Momentarily, my mind switched to a nervous alertness: a sudden déjà vu as I pictured three burly men, dressed in black, appearing at the front counter.

I tentatively walked towards the internal door which led to the front office, hesitant to see who was at the front desk. I peered towards the station foyer and felt relief as I realised my fears were mistaken; it was Maxine, an elderly resident who lived a couple of doors up from the police station. I smiled and greeted her as I approached the counter. 'Here's some fresh scones, just out of the oven.' As Maxine pulled the tea towel back to reveal a tray of golden scones with butter melting down their sides, the delicious aroma of freshly baked scones escaped. 'I thought you would enjoy them,' she said.

I thanked Maxine for her kindness and enquired how her accordion club was getting along. She enthusiastically spoke of recent events, extending her invitation to neighbourhood

officers to join her at an accordion night at her home after fin-
ishing their Saturday late duty. As Maxine left the station I took
the scones through to the rear kitchen. As I had a little nibble I
smiled as I thought, 'Yes, nothing ever happens here.'

APPENDIX: PEELIAN PRINCIPLES

SIR ROBERT PEEL'S PRINCIPLES OF LAW ENFORCEMENT

The principles, which were set out in the General Instructions issued to every new police officer from 1829, were:

1. To prevent crime and disorder, as an alternative to their repression by military force and severity of legal punishment.

2. To recognise always that the power of the police to fulfil their functions and duties is dependent on public approval of their existence, actions and behaviour and on their ability to secure and maintain public respect.

3. To recognise always that to secure and maintain the respect and approval of the public means also the securing of the willing cooperation of the public in the task of securing observance of laws.

4. To recognise always that the extent to which the cooperation of the public can be secured diminishes proportionately the necessity of the use of physical force and compulsion for achieving police objectives.

5. To seek and preserve public favour, not by pandering to public opinion, but by constantly demonstrating absolutely impartial service to law, in complete independence of policy, and without regard to the justice or injustice of the substance of individual laws, by ready offering of individual service and friendship to all members of the public without regard to their wealth or social standing, by ready exercise of courtesy and friendly good humour, and by ready offering of individual sacrifice in protecting and preserving life.

6. To use physical force only when the exercise of persuasion, advice and warning is found to be insufficient to obtain public cooperation to an extent necessary to secure observance of law or to restore order, and to use only the minimum degree of physical force which is necessary on any particular occasion for achieving a police objective.

7. To maintain at all times a relationship with the public that gives reality to the historic tradition that the police are the public and that the public are the police, the police being only members of the public who are paid to give full-time attention to duties which are incumbent on every citizen in the interests of community welfare and existence.

8. To recognise always the need for strict adherence to police-executive functions, and to refrain from even seeming to usurp the powers of the judiciary of avenging individuals or the State, and of authoritatively judging guilt and punishing the guilty.

9. To recognise always that the test of police efficiency is the absence of crime and disorder, and not the visible evidence of police action in dealing with them.

ACKNOWLEDGEMENTS

Writing *Nothing Ever Happens Here* would not have been possible without reference to the many stories, missives and first-hand accounts from former colleagues, residents, friends and family. Throughout the book I have presented people's honestly held views as told, without influence or favour.

I am grateful to my former police colleagues, who were in the public eye each day, striving to keep the community reassured and safe. Their recollection of events were invaluable in shaping the narrative of this book.

I wish also to personally thank Northumbria Police for their openness and transparency, evident in the numerous articles, media releases and factual programmes placed in the public domain at the time of the incident and thereafter. I firmly believe that no police force in the country would have handled the incident better, or secured a more desirable outcome, than Northumbria Police.

Furthermore, the contribution of Rothbury residents, volunteers and key stakeholders was overwhelming as they reflected on their feelings and emotions and the impact Raoul Moat had on their community.

Finally, I am indebted to my family for their patience, love and understanding while I undertook the Herculean task of writing this book, especially my daughter Ella for the many hours spent proofreading in the park during lockdown, following the cancellation of her GCSE exams in 2020.

Thank you for taking the time to read about the Raoul Moat incident from a community, neighbourhood policing and rural Northumberland perspective. As a final footnote, I retired from Northumbria Police in 2017 and embarked on a role in education, supporting our young people in realising their potential and developing their character, which will hopefully serve to strengthen their communities for generations to come.

—Graham Vickers, October 2020